TAGINES
& COUSCOUS

LONDON • NEW YORK

TAGINES
& COUSCOUS

Delicious recipes for Moroccan one-pot cooking

Ghillie Başan

photography by Martin Brigdale and Peter Cassidy

Design and Photographic Art Direction
Steve Painter and Liz Sephton
Senior Commissioning Editor Julia Charles
Production Controller Toby Marshall
Art Director Leslie Harrington
Publishing Director Alison Starling

Photography Martin Brigdale and
Peter Cassidy
Food Stylists Ross Dobson, Bridget
Sargeson and Lucy McKelvie
Prop Styling Helen Trent, Martin Brigdale
and Steve Painter
Indexer Hilary Bird

First published in the United States
in 2010
by Ryland Peters & Small, Inc.
519 Broadway, 5th Floor
New York, NY 10012
www.rylandpeters.com

20 19 18 17 16 15 14 13 12 11

Photography credits
© Martin Brigdale: Pages 4, 5, 132, 133
© Ryland Peters & Small by Martin
Brigdale: Pages 1 above, 2, 3, 14 below
right, 16, 18, 21, 27, 30–35, 40, 43,
46–53, 56–60, 64–68, 72 below left,
75, 78, 82, 86–93, 96–103, 114, 119,
120, 139, 141.
© Ryland Peters & Small by Peter
Cassidy: Pages 1 below, 6, 9–13, 14
above, below left, & below center, 17,
22–24, 28, 36, 38, 39, 44, 45, 54, 55,
63, 70, 71, 72 above & below right, 77,
81, 84, 85, 94, 95, 104–113, 117, 118,
122–130, 135–138, 142, endpapers.

Library of Congress Cataloging-in-
Publication Data

Başan, Ghillie.
    Tagines & couscous : delicious recipes
for Moroccan one-pot cooking / Ghillie
Başan.
        p. cm.
    Includes index.
    ISBN 978-1-84597-948-5
    1. Cookery, Moroccan. 2. One-dish
meals. 3. Stews. 4. Couscous. I. Title.
    TX725.M8B392 2010
    641.5964--dc22

2009041543

Some of the recipes in this book have
been published previously by Ryland
Peters & Small in *Tagine* and *Flavors
of Morocco*.

Notes
• All spoon measurements are level.
• All eggs are large, unless otherwise
specified. Uncooked or partially
cooked eggs should not be served to
the very young, the elderly, those with
a compromised immune system or
pregnant women.
• When a recipe calls for the grated peel
of citrus fruit, buy unwaxed fruit and
wash well before using. If you can only
find treated fruit, scrub well in warm
soapy water and rinse before using.
• Sterlize preserving jars before use.
Wash in hot soapy water and rinse in
boiling water. Place in a large saucepan,
cover with hot water, bring to the boil
and boil, covered, for 15 minutes. Turn
off the heat and leave in the hot water
until using. Invert onto paper towels to
dry. Sterlize lids for 5 minutes, by
boiling. Jars should be filled while hot.
• Ovens should be preheated to the
specified temperature. Recipes in this
book were tested in a regular oven.
If using a fan-assisted oven, follow
the maker's instructions for adjusting
temperatures.

For digital editions visit
rylandpeters.com/apps.php

CONTENTS

the secrets of tagines

Colorful, decorative, scented, and a feast for the senses—the food of Morocco reflects a fascinating mix of the cultures that have left their mark on the region: the indigenous Berbers with their tradition of tagine cooking and couscous; the nomadic Bedouins from the desert who brought dates, milk, and grains; the Moors expelled from Spain who relied heavily on olives and olive oil and brought with them the Andalusian flavors of paprika and herbs; the Sephardic Jews with their preserving techniques employing salt; the Arabs who introduced the sophisticated cuisine from the Middle East; the Ottoman influence of kebabs and pastry making; and finally, the finesse of the French.

The root of Moroccan cooking can be traced back to the indigenous Berber tribes. Steeped in tradition, the rural Berbers are proud of their ancestry. They have lived in North Africa, between Egypt and the western coast of Morocco, as far back as archaeological records go. Originally farmers, living alongside the nomadic Taureg and Bedouin tribes of the desert, the Berbers would have made an impact on the food of the region long before the invasion of the Arabs and, although they had to convert from Christianity to Islam and adopt new religious and culinary customs, they are keen to make the point that they are not of Arab descent. Many rural Berber communities speak their own languages and dialects but those who are literate also speak Arabic and, in some areas, French. Berbers also fiercely uphold some of their own culinary customs, such as the festive pilgrimages, moussems, which are held in tented enclosures where traditional dishes, such as

couscous, are cooked in vast quantities and shared. Another feature of Berber culinary life is the diffa, which is a festive banquet, varying in content in accordance with the wealth of the family, to mark special family occasions such as weddings and births and religious events.

It is Berbers we have to thank for tagines and couscous. A tagine is a glorified stew worthy of poetry—aromatic and syrupy, zesty and spicy, or sweet and fragrant are just some of the words that come to mind. It is a dish of tender meat, fish, or succulent vegetables, simmered to perfection in buttery sauces with fruit, herbs, honey, and chiles. An authentic tagine is in a class of its own and has become a fundamental feature of Moroccan cuisine.

The name "tagine" (sometimes spelled "tajine") is also given to the vessel in which the food is cooked: a shallow, round, earthenware pot with a unique conical lid designed to lock in moisture and flavors. In it, the food cooks gently in a small amount of liquid. The finished dish can either be served piping hot straight from its cooking vessel, or tipped into one of the decorative versions of the pot, glazed in shades of blue and green, to take to the table.

Although originally a Berber dish, the tagine has evolved with the history of the region as waves of Arab and Ottoman invaders, Moorish refugees from Andalusia and French colonialists have left their influences on the cuisine. Classic tagines include combinations of lamb with dried prunes or apricots; chicken with preserved lemon and green olives; duck with dates and honey; and fish cooked with tomatoes, lime, and cilantro. In the modern Maghreb, the Berbers are still renowned for their tasty, pungent tagines made with lots of onions and *smen*, a rancid clarified butter (see page 11) which is very much an acquired taste!

The method employed in tagine cooking also varies from the countryside to the cities. In the north, in cities like Tangier and Casablanca, where the Spanish and French influences are evident, the meat is often browned in butter or oil and the spices and onions are sautéed before adding the rest of the ingredients, whereas Fassi and Marrakchi tagines are prepared by putting all the ingredients together in water and then adding extra butter or *smen* towards the end of the cooking time.

Traditionally, tagines are served as a course on their own, with freshly baked flat breads or crusty bread to mop up the delectable syrupy sauces, and are followed by a mound of couscous. The more modern way is to combine the courses and serve them with an accompanying salad or vegetable side. On festive occasions, the custom is to pile up a huge pyramid of couscous and hollow out the peak to form a well into which the tagine is spooned. However, most earthenware tagines are not big enough to cope with feasts, so large copper pots are often used instead.

The great secret of an authentic tagine is to simmer the ingredients over a low heat, so that everything remains deliciously moist and tender. Meat tagines may be cooked for several hours, the meat simmering gently in a seasoned, fragrant liquid until it is so tender it almost falls off the bone. Generally, dishes of vegetables, pulses or fish do not require long cooking times but still benefit from the tagine method in terms of enhanced taste and texture.

Traditionally, tagines are cooked over a clay stove, or brazier, which is stoked with charcoal to maintain constant heat. Such stoves diffuse the heat around the base of the tagine, enabling the liquid to reduce and thicken without drying out. Wood-burning ovens and open fires are used, too. However, wonderful tagines can also be produced using a modern stovetop or oven. Most authentic tagines have a little hole at the top of the conical lid to release some of the steam, so that it doesn't try to escape at the seam between the base and the lid. If there is no hole, you will probably need at intervals to tilt the lid at an angle to release the steam yourself. When cooking in an oven, it is generally only the base of the tagine that is used.

When it comes to buying a tagine, there are several different types and sizes, as some represent a Berber tribe, a particular village, or a region of Morocco. There are a number of cooking tagines to choose from, but few of them come with a warning about their vulnerability over a conventional gas or electric stovetop. Most of the factory-made vessels, whether they are glazed or not, tend to form hairline cracks when they are placed directly over a gas flame; and they cannot be used on an electric ring. So what do you do? For a glazed earthenware tagine, a heat diffuser is essential, otherwise it is worth splashing out on the durable cast-iron version with a glazed, earthenware lid produced by Le Creuset. Their version looks just like a beautifully authentic glazed tagine but the cast-iron base enables it to be used safely on gas or electric stovetops. A solid, heavy-based casserole dish is a good substitute, as long as you keep the heat very low. But for a tasty, succulent meal, full of flavor and adventure it is well worth attempting to cook with the genuine article.

smen (aged butter)

This pungent butter, used as the primary cooking fat in some tagines, is left to mature in earthenware pots for months, sometimes years! You can substitute it with ghee (clarified butter).

4 sticks unsalted butter, at room temperature

1 tablespoon sea salt

1 tablespoon dried oregano

Makes about 500 g

Soften the butter in a bowl. Boil ⅔ cup water in a saucepan with the salt and oregano to reduce it a little, then strain it directly onto the butter. Stir the butter with a wooden spoon to make sure it is well blended, then let cool.

Knead the butter with your hands to bind it, squeezing out any excess water. Drain well and spoon the butter into a hot, sterilized jar (see note on page 4.) Seal the jar and store it in a cool, dry place for at least 6 weeks.

preserved lemons

Added to many dishes as a refreshing, tangy ingredient or garnish, preserved lemons are essential to the cooking of tagines. You can buy jars of ready-preserved lemons in specialist shops and some larger stores, but it is worth making your own.

10 organic, unwaxed lemons, preferably the small, thin-skinned Meyer variety

10 tablespoons sea salt

freshly squeezed juice of 3–4 lemons

Makes 1 large jar

Wash and dry the lemons and slice the ends off each one. Stand each lemon on one end and make two vertical cuts three-quarters of the way through them, as if cutting them into quarters but keeping the base intact. Stuff 1 tablespoon salt into each lemon and pack them into a large sterilized jar (see note on page 4.) Seal the jar and store the lemons in a cool place for 3–4 days to soften the skins.

Press the lemons down into the jar, so they are even more tightly packed. Pour the lemon juice over the salted lemons, until they are completely covered. Seal the jar again and store it in a cool place for at least 1 month. Rinse the salt off the preserved lemons before using.

chermoula

A distinctive Moroccan marinade, chermoula is often employed in fish dishes as the flavors of chile, ground cumin, and cilantro marry so well and complement the fish perfectly.

2 garlic cloves, chopped

1 teaspoon coarse sea salt

1–2 teaspoons cumin seeds, crushed or ground

1 fresh red chile, seeded and chopped

freshly squeezed juice of 1 lemon

2 tablespoons olive oil

a small bunch of cilantro, roughly chopped and/or a small bunch of flat-leaf parsley, chopped

Makes 1 small pot

To make the chermoula, use a mortar and pestle to pound the garlic and chile with the salt to form a paste. Add the cilantro and parsley leaves and pound to a coarse paste. Beat in the cumin and paprika and bind well with the olive oil and lemon juice (you can whizz all the ingredients together in an electric blender, if you prefer.)

harissa paste

This fiery paste is popular throughout North Africa. It can be served as a condiment, or as a dip for warm crusty bread, and it can be stirred into tagines and couscous to impart its distinctive chile taste. This recipe is for the basic paste, to which other ingredients such as fennel seeds, cilantro, and mint can be added. Jars of ready-prepared harissa are available in some larger stores and specialist retailers but it's easy to make your own.

8 dried red chiles (Horn or New Mexico), seeded

2–3 garlic cloves, finely chopped

½ teaspoon sea salt

1 teaspoon ground cumin

1 teaspoon ground coriander

4 tablespoons olive oil

Makes about 4 tablespoons

Put the chiles in a bowl and pour over enough warm water to cover them. Leave them to soak for 1 hour. Drain and squeeze out any excess water. Using a mortar and pestle, pound them to a paste with the garlic and salt (or whizz them in an electric mixer.) Beat in the cumin and ground coriander and bind with the olive oil.

Store the harissa in a sealed jar in the refrigerator with a thin layer of olive oil poured on top. It will keep well for about 1 month.

ras-el-hanout

There is no one recipe for *ras-el-hanout*, a lovely pungent spice mix, packed with strong Indian aromas of cinnamon, cloves, and ginger combined with local African roots and the delicate, perfumed notes of rosebuds. Every family has its own favorite blend. Some of the spices are available only in the Maghreb, so if your tagine recipe calls for this flavoring your easiest solution is to select one of the ready-prepared spice mixes available in Middle Eastern and African stores—you can order a moist, aromatic ras-al-hanout online from spice specialists Zamouri Spices at www.zamourispices.com. Alternatively, you could try this version.

◆ ◆

1 teaspoon black peppercorns

1 teaspoon cloves

1 teaspoon aniseeds

1 teaspoon nigella seeds

1 teaspoon allspice berries

1 teaspoon cardamom seeds

2 teaspoons ground ginger

2 teaspoons ground turmeric

2 teaspoons coriander seeds

2 pieces mace

2 pieces cinnamon bark

2 teaspoons dried mint

1 dried red chile

1 teaspoon dried lavender

6 dried rosebuds, broken up

Makes about 4–5 tablespoons

Using a mortar and pestle, or an electric blender, grind together all the spices to form a coarse powder.

Stir in the lavender and rose petals and tip the mixture into an airtight container.

You can store this spice mix for up to 6 months if you keep it in a cool cupboard and well away from direct sunlight.

traditional lamb tagines

lamb tagine with prunes, apricots, and honey

A classic lamb tagine, sweetened with honey and fruit, is the perfect introduction to the tastes of Morocco. Traditionally, this aromatic dish is served with bread to mop up the syrupy sauce. To balance the sweetness, you could also serve a crunchy salad of finely shredded carrot, onions, and cabbage or bell peppers, spiked with chile.

* *

1–2 tablespoons ghee, or 1 tablespoon olive oil plus a pat of butter

2 tablespoons blanched almonds

2 red onions, finely chopped

2–3 garlic cloves, finely chopped

a thumb-size piece of fresh ginger, peeled and chopped

a pinch of saffron threads

2 cinnamon sticks

1–2 teaspoons coriander seeds, crushed

1 lb. boned lamb, from the shoulder, leg, or shanks, trimmed and cubed

12 dried pitted prunes, soaked for 1 hour and drained

6 dried pitted apricots, soaked for 1 hour and drained

3–4 strips orange peel

1–2 tablespoons dark, runny honey

leaves from a small bunch of cilantro, finely chopped

sea salt and freshly ground black pepper

crusty bread, to serve

Serves 4–6

Heat the ghee in a tagine or heavy-based casserole dish, stir in the almonds and cook until they turn golden. Add the onions and garlic and sauté until they begin to color. Stir in the ginger, saffron, cinnamon sticks, and coriander seeds. Toss in the lamb, making sure it is coated in the onion and spices, and sauté for 1–2 minutes.

Pour in enough water to just cover the meat and bring it to a boil. Reduce the heat, cover the tagine or casserole and simmer for about 1 hour, until the meat is tender. Add the prunes, apricots, and orange peel, cover the tagine again, and simmer for a further 15–20 minutes. Stir in the honey, season with salt and pepper to taste, cover and simmer for a further 10 minutes. Make sure there is enough liquid in the pot, as you want the sauce to be syrupy and slightly caramelized, but not too dry—add a little more water if necessary.

Stir in some of the cilantro and reserve the rest to sprinkle over the top of the dish. Serve immediately with crusty bread.

lamb tagine with dates, almonds, and pistachios

In Arab culture, dates are an age-old source of nutrition and natural sugar; nomads could survive in the desert with dates alone for nourishment. As the fruit is regarded as special, it is often added to festive grain dishes and stews. This slightly sticky date and nut tagine is a favorite at weddings and other family feasts.

◆ ◆

2–3 tablespoons ghee, or 1 tablespoon olive oil plus a pat of butter

2 onions, finely chopped

1–2 teaspoons ground turmeric

1 teaspoon ground ginger

2 teaspoons ground cinnamon

2 lbs. lean lamb, from the shoulder, neck, or leg, cut into bite-size pieces

8 oz. ready-to-eat pitted dates

1 tablespoon dark, runny honey

1 tablespoon olive oil

a pat of butter

2–3 tablespoons blanched almonds

2 tablespoons shelled pistachios

leaves from a small bunch of fresh flat-leaf parsley, finely chopped

sea salt and freshly ground black pepper

Plain, Buttery Couscous (see page 108), to serve

Serves 4

Heat the ghee in a tagine or heavy-based casserole dish. Stir in the onions and sauté until golden brown. Stir in the turmeric, ginger, and cinnamon. Toss in the meat, making sure it is coated in the spice mixture. Pour in enough water to almost cover the meat and bring it to a boil. Reduce the heat, cover with a lid, and simmer gently for roughly 1½ hours.

Add the dates and stir in the honey. Cover with a lid again and simmer for another 30 minutes. Season with salt and lots of black pepper.

Heat the olive oil with the butter in a small pan. Stir in the almonds and pistachios and cook until they begin to turn golden brown.

Scatter the toasted nuts over the lamb and dates and sprinkle with the flat-leaf parsley. Serve with Plain, Buttery Couscous and a sharp, crunchy salad with preserved lemon to cut the sweetness.

lamb tagine with shallots and dates

Commonly known as the "bread of the desert" the Arabs and the Berbers treat dates as a sacred food source as they and their ancestors have survived off them for generations, even when there has been little else to eat. They also symbolize hospitality and prosperity, so they are offered to guests and they are popped into numerous tagines and couscous dishes.

• •

3 tablespoons ghee, or 2 tablespoons olive oil plus a pat of butter

1½ lbs. lean boned lamb, from the shoulder or neck, trimmed and cut into bite-size pieces

12 shallots, peeled and left whole

4–6 garlic cloves, peeled and left whole

2 teaspoons ground turmeric

2 cinnamon sticks

1–2 tablespoons dark, runny honey

8 oz. ready-to-eat pitted dates

1–2 tablespoons sesame seeds, toasted

sea salt and freshly ground black pepper

crusty bread or Plain, Buttery Couscous (see page 108), to serve

Serves 4–6

Heat the ghee in a tagine or heavy-based casserole dish. Toss in the lamb and brown it all over. Using a slotted spoon, remove the meat from the tagine and set aside. Add the shallots and garlic to the tagine and sauté, stirring occasionally, until they begin to color.

Add the turmeric and cinnamon sticks and return the meat to the tagine. Pour in just enough water to cover the meat then bring it to a boil. Reduce the heat, cover with the lid and simmer for about 1 hour, giving it a stir from time to time.

Stir in the honey and season with salt and plenty of black pepper. Add the dates, replace the lid, and cook for a further 25–30 minutes.

Sprinkle with the toasted sesame seeds and serve with crusty bread or Plain, Buttery Couscous.

baked lamb tagine with quinces, figs, and honey

In this festive dish, a shoulder of lamb is marinated in chermoula—a delicious Moroccan herb and spice mix—and baked slowly. If you have difficulty sourcing quinces, you can use sharp green apples or pears instead.

◆ ◆

3½ lbs. shoulder of lamb on the bone

1 quantity of Chermoula
(see page 12)

2 tablespoons ghee, or 1 tablespoon
olive oil plus a pat of butter

2 red onions, cut into wedges

8 oz. ready-to-eat pitted prunes

8 oz. ready-to-eat dried figs, or
fresh figs, halved

3 tablespoons butter

2 fresh quinces, quartered and cored
(keep soaked in water with a squeeze
of lemon until ready to use)

2–3 tablespoons orange flower water

2 tablespoons dark, runny honey

leaves from a small bunch of fresh
flat-leaf parsley, chopped

leaves from a small bunch of cilantro,
chopped

Plain, Buttery Couscous (see page
108) or roasted potatoes, to serve

Serves 4–6

Cut small incisions in the shoulder of lamb with a sharp knife and rub the chermoula well into the meat. Cover and leave in the refrigerator for at least 6 hours, or overnight.

Preheat the oven to 350°F.

Heat the ghee in a tagine or heavy-based casserole dish, add the lamb and brown it all over. Transfer the meat to a plate. Stir the onions and any leftover chermoula into the ghee. Add the prunes and if using dried figs add them at this stage. Pour in 1¼ cups water and put the lamb back into the tagine. Cover with the lid and put the tagine in the oven for about 2 hours.

Towards the end of the cooking time, melt the butter in a heavy-based pan, toss in the quinces and sauté until golden brown. Remove the tagine from the oven and place the golden quince around the meat (if using fresh figs, add them at this stage.) Splash the orange flower water over the lamb and drizzle the honey over the meat and the fruit. Return the tagine to the oven for a further 25–30 minutes, until the meat and fruit are nicely browned and the lamb is so tender it almost falls off the bone.

Sprinkle the parsley and cilantro over the top and serve with Plain, Buttery Couscous or roasted potatoes.

lamb tagine with chestnuts, saffron, and pomegranate seeds

This is a lovely winter dish, decorated with jewel-like ruby-red pomegranate seeds. Whole, meaty chestnuts are often used in Arab-influenced culinary cultures as a substitute for potatoes. You can use freshly roasted nuts or ready-peeled, vacuum-packed or frozen chestnuts.

• •

2 tablespoons ghee, or 1 tablespoon olive oil plus a pat of butter

2 onions, finely chopped

4 garlic cloves, finely chopped

thumb-size piece of fresh ginger, peeled and finely chopped or shredded

a pinch of saffron threads

1–2 cinnamon sticks

2 lbs. lean lamb, from the shoulder or leg, cut into bite-size pieces

8 oz. peeled chestnuts

1–2 tablespoons dark, runny honey

seeds of 1 pomegranate, pith removed

leaves from a small bunch of fresh mint, chopped

leaves from a small bunch of cilantro, chopped

sea salt and freshly ground black pepper

crusty bread or Plain, Buttery Couscous (see page 108), to serve

Serves 4

Heat the ghee in a tagine or heavy-based casserole dish. Stir in the onions, garlic, and ginger and sauté until they begin to color. Add the saffron and cinnamon sticks, and toss in the lamb. Pour in enough water to almost cover the meat and bring it to a boil. Reduce the heat, cover with a lid, and simmer gently for about 1 hour.

Add the chestnuts and stir in the honey. Cover with the lid again and cook gently for a further 30 minutes, until the meat is very tender.

Season to taste with salt and plenty of black pepper and then toss in some of the pomegranate seeds, mint, and cilantro. Sprinkle the remaining pomegranate seeds and herbs over the lamb, and serve with crusty bread or Plain, Buttery Couscous.

See photograph on page 31.

tfaia tagine with onions, browned almonds, and eggs

Originally from Andalusia, tfaia tagines are popular in northern Morocco, particularly in Tangier. Their trademark is a pungent, nutty flavor that emanates from matured, clarified butter called *smen* which is an acquired taste for some people. The recipe works just as well with ghee, which is ordinary clarified butter.

• •

*1–2 tablespoons ghee or smen
(see page 11)*

2 garlic cloves, crushed

1 teaspoon ground ginger

1 teaspoon ground coriander

*1 teaspoon saffron threads, ground
with a pinch of salt*

2 lbs. lamb cutlets

2 onions, finely chopped

6 oz. black Kalamata olives, pitted

*2 preserved lemons (see page 11),
cut into quarters*

*leaves from a small bunch of cilantro,
chopped*

*sea salt and freshly ground
black pepper*

To serve:

4 eggs

*½ teaspoon ground saffron, or
a pinch of saffron threads*

½ tablespoon ghee or butter

2 tablespoons blanched almonds

crusty bread

Serves 4

Melt the ghee in a tagine or heavy-based casserole dish. Stir in the garlic, ginger, ground coriander, and saffron, and roll the lamb cutlets in the mixture. Sprinkle the onions over the cutlets and pour in just enough water to cover the meat. Bring the water to a boil, reduce the heat, cover with a lid, and cook gently for about 1½ hours.

Add the olives and lemons and cook, uncovered, for about another 20 minutes to reduce the sauce. Season well with plenty of salt and black pepper and toss in the chopped cilantro.

Meanwhile, boil the eggs in their shells for about 4 minutes, so that the yolk is just firm, and shell them. Dissolve the saffron in 2 tablespoons warm water and roll the eggs in the yellow liquid to color them. Cut the eggs in half lengthwise.

In a skillet, melt the ghee and stir in the almonds until golden brown. Sprinkle the toasted almonds over the tagine and arrange the eggs around the edge. Serve immediately with crusty bread.

summer tagine of lamb, zucchini, bell peppers, and mint

Summer tagines using seasonal vegetables are often quite light and colorful. Other vegetables that might be added to this tagine include tomatoes, eggplant, and peas. This dish is particularly good served with wedges of lemon to squeeze over it, or with finely shredded preserved lemon sprinkled over the top.

• •

3–4 tablespoons olive oil

1 onion, roughly chopped

4 garlic cloves, roughly chopped

1 teaspoon cumin seeds

1 teaspoon coriander seeds

1 teaspoon dried mint

thumb-size piece of fresh ginger, peeled and finely chopped or grated

1½ lbs. lean lamb, from the shoulder or leg, cut into bite-size pieces

2 small zucchini, sliced thickly on the diagonal

1 red or yellow bell pepper, seeded and cut into thick strips

4 tomatoes, skinned, seeded, and cut into chunks

leaves from a small bunch of fresh flat-leaf parsley, roughly chopped

leaves from a small bunch of fresh mint, roughly chopped

sea salt and freshly ground black pepper

1 lemon, cut into quarters, to serve

Serves 4–6

Heat the olive oil in a tagine or heavy-based casserole dish. Stir in the onion, garlic, cumin and coriander seeds, dried mint, and ginger. Once the onions begin to soften, toss in the meat and pour in enough water to just cover it. Bring the water to a boil, reduce the heat, cover with a lid, and cook gently for about 1½ hours.

Season the cooking juices with salt and pepper. Add the zucchini, bell pepper, and tomatoes, tucking them around the meat (add a little more water if necessary.) Cover with a lid again and cook for about 15 minutes, until the zucchini and bell pepper are cooked but retain a little bite.

Toss in some of the chopped parsley and mint, sprinkle the rest over the top and serve immediately with lemon wedges on the side to squeeze over the dish.

lamb k'dra with sweet potatoes and okra

This is a Berber dish which is often prepared with large cuts of meat, such as shanks, knuckle, or sheeps' heads, which are removed at the end of the cooking and arranged around a mound of couscous. The vegetables are arranged on top and the cooking broth is served separately to spoon over the dish.

• •

6–8 lamb shanks, trimmed and cut into bite-size pieces

6 onions, halved lengthwise and sliced crosswise

a pinch of saffron threads

2 cinnamon sticks

1 teaspoon ground black pepper

2 sweet potatoes, peeled, halved lengthwise, and thickly sliced

2 tablespoons ghee, smen (see page 11), or butter

8 oz. fresh okra

freshly squeezed juice of 1 lemon

sea salt

crusty bread or Plain, Buttery Couscous (see page 108), to serve

Serves 6–8

Put the lamb in a tagine or large heavy-based casserole dish with half of the onions, saffron, cinnamon sticks, and black pepper. Pour in enough water to cover the meat and bring it to a boil. Reduce the heat, cover with a lid, and simmer gently for about 1½ hours (top up with water if necessary.)

Add the sweet potatoes, ghee, and the rest of the onions. Simmer for a further 20–25 minutes, until the potatoes are tender. Meanwhile, toss the okra in the lemon juice, leave for 10 minutes, then drain. Add the okra to the casserole dish and simmer for a further 5–10 minutes, until the okra is cooked through but still retains a crunch.

Season to taste with salt and serve with crusty bread or Plain, Buttery Couscous.

beef, kefta, and sausage tagines

beef tagine with beets and oranges

Earthy and fruity, with a hint of ginger, this tagine is a good winter warmer. It can be made with either fresh or pre-cooked beets. You could serve it with roasted butternut squash and a mound of Plain, Buttery Couscous tossed with pistachios.

• •

1–2 tablespoons ghee, or 1 tablespoon olive oil plus a pat of butter

3–4 garlic cloves, crushed

1 red onion, halved lengthwise and sliced with the grain

1½ inch piece of fresh ginger, peeled and finely chopped or grated

1 red chile, seeded and sliced

2 teaspoons coriander seeds, crushed

2 cinnamon sticks

3–4 beets, peeled and quartered

1 lb. lean beef, cut into bite-size cubes or strips

2 thin-skinned oranges, cut into segments

1 tablespoon dark, runny honey

1–2 tablespoons orange flower water

a pat of butter

2–3 tablespoons shelled pistachios

leaves from a small bunch of fresh flat-leaf parsley, roughly chopped

sea salt and freshly ground black pepper

Plain, Buttery Couscous (see page 108), to serve

Serves 4–6

Melt the ghee in a tagine or heavy-based casserole dish, add the garlic, onion, and ginger and stir until they begin to color. Add the chile, coriander seeds, and cinnamon sticks. Add the beets and sauté for 2–3 minutes. Toss in the beef and sauté for 1 minute. Pour in enough water to almost cover the beef and beets and bring to a boil. Reduce the heat, cover with a lid and simmer for 1 hour, until the meat is very tender.

Add the orange segments, honey, and orange flower water to the tagine and season to taste with salt and pepper. Cover with the lid and cook for a further 10–15 minutes.

Melt the butter in a small saucepan and toss in the pistachios, stirring them over medium heat until they turn golden brown. Sprinkle them over the tagine along with the flat-leaf parsley and serve immediately.

beef tagine with sweet potatoes, peas, ginger, and ras-el-hanout

This fairly fiery dish is laced with the powerful flavors and aromas of ras-el-hanout, a traditional spice mix. Regional variations use turnip, yam, pumpkin, or butternut squash instead of sweet potatoes. It is best served with chunks of crusty bread and cooling yogurt or a glass of mint tea.

* *

*2 tablespoons ghee or smen
(see page 11), or 1 tablespoon olive oil
plus a pat of butter*

*1½ inch piece of fresh ginger, peeled
and finely shredded*

1 onion, finely chopped

2 lbs. lean beef, cut into bite-size pieces

*1–2 teaspoons ras-el-hanout
(see page 15)*

2 sweet potatoes, peeled and cubed

1 lb. fresh or frozen peas

*2–3 tomatoes, skinned, seeded,
and chopped*

*1 preserved lemon (see page 11),
finely shredded or chopped*

*leaves from a small bunch of cilantro,
finely chopped*

*sea salt and freshly ground
black pepper*

*crusty bread and plain yogurt,
to serve*

Serves 4

Heat the ghee in a tagine or heavy-based casserole dish. Add in the ginger and onion and sauté until soft. Toss in the beef and sear it on all sides, then stir in the ras-el-hanout. Pour in enough water to just cover the meat and bring it to a boil. Reduce the heat, cover with the lid and cook gently for about 40 minutes.

Add the sweet potato to the tagine, season to taste with salt and pepper, cover with the lid, and cook gently for a further 20 minutes, until the meat is tender. Toss in the peas and tomatoes, cover with the lid and cook for 5–10 minutes.

Sprinkle the preserved lemon and chopped cilantro over the top and serve immediately with crusty bread and plain yogurt.

kefta tagine with eggs and roasted cumin

Variations of this great street dish can be found throughout the Maghreb. It is also often prepared as a snack in the home. In many households, kefta (poached meatballs) are prepared in batches and stored in the refrigerator. Kefta are usually quite fiery, so serve them with plenty of good bread and plain yogurt to temper their hotness.

• •

For the kefta:

½ lb. finely ground lamb

1 onion, finely chopped

1 teaspoon dried mint

*1–2 teaspoons ras-el-hanout
(see page 15)*

½ teaspoon cayenne pepper

*leaves from a small bunch of fresh
flat-leaf parsley, finely chopped*

*sea salt and freshly ground
black pepper*

1 tablespoon butter

¼–½ teaspoon salt

*1 teaspoon cayenne pepper or
½ teaspoon dried hot pepper flakes*

4 eggs

*1–2 teaspoons cumin seeds,
dry-roasted and ground*

*leaves from a small bunch of fresh
flat-leaf parsley, roughly chopped*

*crusty bread and plain yogurt,
to serve*

Serves 4

To make the kefta, put the ground lamb, onion, mint, ras-el-hanout, cayenne pepper, and parsley in a bowl. Season to taste with salt and pepper and mix well together. Using your hands, knead the mixture and mould it into small walnut-size balls, so that you end up with about 12 balls.

Fill a tagine or heavy-based casserole dish with water and bring it to a boil. Carefully drop in the kefta, a few at a time, and poach them for about 10 minutes, turning them so that they are cooked on all sides. Remove them with a slotted spoon and drain on paper towels. Reserve roughly 1¼ cups of the cooking liquid. (If not using the kefta immediately, transfer them to a plate to cool and store covered in the refrigerator for 2–3 days.)

Add the butter to the reserved cooking liquid in the tagine and bring the mixture to a boil. Stir in the salt and cayenne pepper and drop in the poached kefta. Cook over high heat until almost all the liquid has evaporated. Carefully crack the eggs around the kefta, cover with a lid, and leave the eggs to cook in the sauce and steam until they are just set.

Sprinkle the roasted cumin and chopped parsley over the top of the dish and serve immediately with crusty bread and plain yogurt.

spicy kefta tagine with lemon

Kefta tagines don't require long cooking times as generally the sauce is made first and the meatballs are poached in it. This recipe is light and lemony and delicious served with Plain, Buttery Couscous tossed with chile and herbs and leafy salad greens.

* *

For the kefta:

1 lb. finely ground beef or lamb

1 onion, finely chopped or grated

leaves from a small bunch of fresh flat-leaf parsley, finely chopped

1–2 teaspoons ground cinnamon

1 teaspoon ground cumin

1 teaspoon ground coriander

½ teaspoon cayenne pepper

sea salt and freshly ground black pepper

1 tablespoon each olive oil and butter

1 onion, roughly chopped

2–3 garlic cloves, halved and crushed

a thumb-size piece of fresh ginger, peeled and finely chopped

1 red chile, thinly sliced

2 teaspoons ground turmeric

leaves from a small bunch of cilantro, chopped

leaves from a small bunch of fresh mint, chopped

freshly squeezed juice of 1 lemon

1 lemon, cut into wedges, pips removed

Plain, Buttery Couscous (see page 108), tossed with finely chopped red chile and fresh green herbs

Serves 4–6

To make the kefta, pound the ground meat with your knuckles in a bowl. Using your hands, lift up the lump of ground meat and slap it back down into the bowl. Add the onion, parsley, cinnamon, cumin, coriander, and cayenne, and season to taste with salt and black pepper. Using your hands, mix the ingredients together and knead well, pounding the mixture for a few minutes. Take pieces of the mixture and shape them into little walnut-size balls, so that you end up with about 16 kefta. (These can be made ahead of time and kept in the refrigerator for 2–3 days.)

Heat the oil and butter in a tagine or heavy-based casserole dish. Stir in the onion, garlic, ginger, and chile and sauté until they begin to brown. Add the turmeric and half the cilantro and mint, and pour in 1¼ cups water. Bring to a boil, reduce the heat and simmer, covered, for 10 minutes. Carefully place the kefta in the liquid, cover and poach for about 15 minutes, rolling them in the liquid from time to time so they are cooked well on all sides. Pour over the lemon juice, season the liquid with salt and tuck the lemon segments around the kefta. Poach for a further 10 minutes.

Sprinkle with the remaining cilantro and mint and serve with Plain, Buttery Couscous tossed with chile and herbs and leafy salad greens, if liked.

chickpea and chorizo tagine with bay leaves, paprika, and sage

This is a classic, Spanish-influenced peasant dish, which is often eaten on its own with yogurt and bread, but is also served with grilled or roasted meats. Either chorizo or Moroccan merguez sausages can be used, as both impart their spicy flavors to the dish. For a meatless version, just omit the sausage, as the chickpeas are extremely tasty on their own.

* *

1 cup dried chickpeas, soaked overnight in plenty of water

2–3 tablespoons olive oil

2 red onions, cut in half lengthwise, halved crosswise, and sliced with the grain

2 garlic cloves, chopped

1 thin chorizo, roughly 8 inches long, sliced on the diagonal, or 1 lb. merguez sausages

2–3 fresh bay leaves

several sprigs of fresh thyme

1–2 teaspoons Spanish smoked paprika (pimentòn)

leaves from a small bunch of fresh sage, shredded

freshly squeezed juice of 1 lemon

sea salt and freshly ground black pepper

warmed flat breads and plain yogurt, to serve

Serves 4

Drain the chickpeas, put them in a large saucepan and cover with plenty of water. Bring the water to a boil, reduce the heat, and simmer for roughly 45 minutes or until the chickpeas are soft but still have a bite to them. Drain well and refresh under cold running water. Remove any loose skins and discard them.

Heat the olive oil in a tagine or heavy-based casserole dish. Stir in the onions and garlic and sauté until they begin to color. Add the chorizo, bay leaves, and thyme and sauté until lightly browned. Toss in the chickpeas, add the paprika, and cover with a lid. Cook gently for 10–15 minutes, to allow the flavors to mingle.

Add in the sage leaves and lemon juice and gently toss. Season to taste with salt and pepper and serve hot with warmed flat breads and plain yogurt.

chorizo tagine with lentils and fenugreek

This is very simple yet delicious peasant food. Prepared with locally-cured, spicy Moroccan merguez sausages or chorizo and lentils or beans, it is a satisfying dish, best served with flat breads and a generous dollop of creamy yogurt.

• •

2 tablespoons olive oil or ghee

2 onions, chopped

2 garlic cloves, chopped

1 lb. chorizo or merguez sausage, thickly sliced

2 teaspoons ground turmeric

2 teaspoons ground fenugreek

1 cup brown lentils

14-oz. can chopped tomatoes

2 teaspoons sugar

leaves from a bunch of cilantro, roughly chopped (reserve some to garnish)

sea salt and freshly ground black pepper

warmed flat breads and plain yogurt, to serve

Serves 4–6

Heat the oil in a tagine or heavy-based casserole dish. Add the onions and garlic and sauté until they begin to color. Toss in the chorizo slices and sauté for 1–2 minutes just to flavor the oil. Stir in the turmeric and fenugreek and add the lentils, making sure they are well coated with the spices.

Add the tomatoes with the sugar and pour in enough water to cover the lentils by 1 inch. Bring the liquid to a boil, reduce the heat, put on the lid and cook gently for about 25 minutes, adding more water if necessary, until the lentils are tender but not mushy.

Toss in the cilantro and season to taste with salt and pepper. Scatter the rest of the cilantro over the top and serve with warmed flat breads and plain yogurt.

chicken and duck tagines

chicken tagine with preserved lemon, green olives, and thyme

Preserved lemon and cracked green olives are two of the principal ingredients of traditional Moroccan cooking. You can buy the olives at Middle Eastern and North African stores. The tagine can be made with chicken joints or a whole chicken. Serve with Plain, Buttery couscous and leafy salad greens or steamed carrots tossed with fresh mint.

* *

8–10 chicken thighs or 4 whole legs

2 tablespoons ghee or 1 tablespoon olive oil plus a pat of butter

2 preserved lemons (see page 11), cut into strips

6 oz. cracked green olives

1–2 teaspoons dried thyme or oregano

Plain, Buttery Couscous (see page 108), to serve

For the marinade:

1 onion, grated

3 garlic cloves, crushed

a 1-inch piece of fresh ginger, peeled and grated

leaves from a small bunch of cilantro, finely chopped

a pinch of saffron threads

freshly squeezed juice of 1 lemon

1 teaspoon coarse sea salt

3–4 tablespoons olive oil

sea salt and freshly ground black pepper

Serves 4

First make the marinade. Mix together all the ingredients together in a small bowl. Put the chicken thighs or legs in a shallow dish and coat them in the marinade, rubbing it into the skin. Cover and chill in the refrigerator for 1–2 hours.

Heat the olive oil with the butter in a tagine or heavy-based casserole dish. Remove the chicken pieces from the marinade and brown them in the oil. Pour over the marinade that is left in the dish and add enough water to come halfway up the sides of the chicken pieces. Bring the water to a boil, reduce the heat, cover and simmer for about 45 minutes, turning the chicken from time to time.

Add the preserved lemon, olives, and half the thyme to the tagine. Cover and simmer for a further 15–20 minutes. Season to taste with salt and pepper and sprinkle the remaining thyme over the top. Serve with Plain, Buttery Couscous and steamed carrots tossed with fresh mint, if liked.

chicken tagine with harissa, artichokes, and green grapes

With the tangy notes of preserved lemon combined with the sweet grapes, this tagine is deliciously refreshing and is best accompanied by warmed flat breads. This recipe uses ready-prepared artichoke hearts which are available jarred or frozen.

• •

4 chicken breasts, cut into thick strips or chunks

2 tablespoons olive oil

2 onions, halved lengthwise and sliced with the grain

½ preserved lemon (see page 11), thinly sliced

1–2 teaspoons sugar

1–2 teaspoons harissa paste (see page 12)

2 teaspoons tomato paste

1¼ cups chicken stock or water

13-oz. jar artichoke hearts, drained, rinsed, and halved

16 green grapes, halved lengthwise

leaves from a bunch of cilantro, coarsely chopped

sea salt and freshly ground black pepper

warmed flat breads, to serve

For the marinade:

2 garlic cloves, crushed

1 teaspoon ground turmeric

freshly squeezed juice of 1 lemon

1 tablespoon olive oil

Serves 4

First, make the marinade. Mix all the ingredients together in a large bowl. Add the chicken breasts to the bowl and toss them in the mixture, then cover and leave in the refrigerator to marinate for 1–2 hours.

Heat the oil in a tagine or heavy-based casserole dish. Add the onions, preserved lemon, and sugar and sauté for 2–3 minutes, until slightly caramelized. Toss in the marinated chicken, then add the harissa and tomato paste. Pour in the stock and bring it to a boil. Reduce the heat, cover and simmer gently for 15 minutes.

Add the artichoke hearts, cover and cook for a further 5 minutes. Add the grapes with some of the cilantro and season to taste with salt and pepper. Sprinkle with the remaining cilantro and serve with warmed flat breads and leafy salad greens, if liked.

spicy chicken tagine with apricots, rosemary, and ginger

This tagine is both fruity and spicy, and the rosemary and ginger give it a delightful aroma. It can also be made with chicken joints or pigeon breasts, pheasant or duck, and needs only Plain, Buttery Couscous and leafy salad greens to accompany it.

◆ ◆

2 tablespoons olive oil plus a pat of butter

1 onion, finely chopped

3 fresh rosemary sprigs, 1 finely chopped, the other 2 cut in half

1½ inch piece of fresh ginger, peeled and finely chopped

2 fresh red chiles, seeded and finely chopped

1–2 cinnamon sticks

8 chicken thighs

6 oz. ready-to-eat dried apricots

2 tablespoons clear, runny honey

14-oz. can plum tomatoes with juice

sea salt and freshly ground black pepper

leaves from a small bunch of fresh green or purple basil

Plain, Buttery Couscous (see page 108), to serve

Serves 4

Heat the oil and butter in a tagine or heavy-based casserole dish. Add the onion, chopped rosemary, ginger, and chiles and sauté until the onion begins to soften.

Stir in the halved rosemary sprigs and the cinnamon sticks. Add the chicken thighs and brown them on both sides. Toss in the apricots with the honey, then stir in the plum tomatoes with their juice. (Add a little water if necessary, to ensure there is enough liquid to cover the base of the tagine and submerge the apricots.) Bring the liquid to a boil, then reduce the heat. Cover and simmer gently for 35–40 minutes, until the chicken is cooked through.

Season to taste with salt and pepper. Shred the larger basil leaves and leave the small ones intact. Sprinkle them over the chicken and serve with Plain, Buttery Couscous and leafy salad greens, if liked.

chicken k'dra with chickpeas, raisins, and red bell peppers

A Moroccan k'dra is a stew cooked in smen, the traditional fermented butter, in a large copper pot (a k'dra). The other feature of a k'dra is the large quantity of onions used in the dish. It is best served on its own with a little bread, and some wedges of lemon to squeeze over it.

◆ ◆

1 chicken, about 3 lbs., jointed into 6 pieces

1¼ cups dried chickpeas, soaked overnight in plenty of water and drained

6 onions, finely chopped

1–2 cinnamon sticks

2 pinches of saffron threads

1 teaspoon each of sea salt and freshly ground black pepper

2 red bell peppers

3–4 tablespoons olive oil

3–4 tablespoons raisins

2 tablespoons ghee, smen (see page 11), or butter

leaves from a bunch of fresh flat-leaf parsley, finely chopped

lemon wedges, to serve

crusty bread, to serve

Serves 4–6

Put the chicken in a large heavy-based casserole dish. Add the chickpeas, 2 tablespoons of the chopped onion, cinnamon sticks, and saffron and season with salt and pepper. Pour in enough water to cover the chicken and chickpeas by about 1 inch and bring to a boil. Cover, reduce the heat, and simmer gently for about 1 hour, checking the water level occasionally.

Meanwhile, preheat the oven to 350°F. Put the bell peppers in a baking dish and pour over the oil. Bake in the preheated oven for about 30 minutes, until tender and the skin has buckled slightly. Remove from the oven and leave until cool enough to handle. Peel the skin off the peppers, cut in half lengthwise, remove the stalk and seeds and cut the flesh into strips. Set aside.

Check the chicken and chickpeas, both of which should be tender, and add the rest of the onions with the raisins, butter, and half of the parsley. Cover and cook gently for a further 40 minutes, until the onions have almost formed a purée and there is very little liquid left in the casserole dish.

Arrange the chicken joints on a serving dish and spoon the chickpea mixture around them. Scatter the strips of bell pepper over the top and serve with lemon wedges and crusty bread or Plain, Buttery Couscous.

chicken k'dra with turnips and chickpeas

Traditionally cooked in a large copper pot, k'dra dishes are often packed with plenty of vegetables and legumes to create a hearty, filling dish for a big family or a large gathering of people.

* *

2 lbs. chicken thighs

1–2 tablespoons ground turmeric

2–3 tablespoons olive oil plus
a pat of butter

2 onions, coarsely chopped

4 garlic cloves, chopped

2–3 teaspoons coriander seeds

1 cup dried chickpeas, soaked
overnight in plenty of water
and drained

8 baby turnips, halved

1 tablespoon ghee or butter, melted
(optional)

leaves from a bunch of fresh
flat-leaf parsley, coarsely chopped

sea salt and freshly ground
black pepper

crusty bread, to serve

Serves 4–6

Trim the chicken thighs and rub them with the ground turmeric. Set aside.

Heat the oil and butter in a large copper pot, or heavy-based saucepan. Add the onions, garlic, and coriander seeds and stir until they begin to color.

Add the chicken thighs and brown lightly, then toss in the chickpeas and cover with 3½ cups water. Bring to a boil, reduce the heat, cover and simmer for about 45 minutes, until the chicken and chickpeas are tender.

Add the turnips and a little extra water if necessary and cook for a further 10–15 minutes, depending on the type of turnip, until cooked but still firm. Season to taste with salt and pepper, pour over the melted ghee, if using, and garnish with the chopped parsley. Serve with crusty bread.

tagine of duck breasts with dates, honey, and orange flower water

This traditional Moorish dish appears in various guises throughout the Arab-influenced world. Poultry cooked with dates and honey is probably one of the most ancient culinary combinations and the finished dish is deliciously succulent. You can substitute the duck with chicken, pigeon, or poussins, if you prefer.

* *

a 1-inch piece of fresh ginger, peeled and chopped

2–3 garlic cloves, chopped

2–3 tablespoons olive oil plus a pat of butter

2 cinnamon sticks

4 duck breasts, on the bone

2–3 tablespoons clear, runny honey

1 cup ready-to-eat pitted dates

1–2 tablespoons orange flower water

sea salt and freshly ground black pepper

1 tablespoon butter

2–3 tablespoons blanched almonds

Plain, Buttery Couscous (see page 108) tossed with finely chopped preserved lemon (see page 11) and fresh green herbs, to serve

Serves 4

Using a mortar and pestle, pound the ginger and garlic to a paste. Heat the olive oil and butter in a tagine or heavy-based casserole dish, then stir in the ginger-garlic paste and the cinnamon sticks. Once the mixture begins to color, add the duck breasts and brown the skin.

Stir in the honey and tuck the dates around the duck. Add enough water (the amount will vary according to the size of your tagine) to cover the base of the tagine and to come about one-third of the way up the duck breasts. Bring to a boil, reduce the heat and cover. Cook gently for about 25 minutes.

Add the orange flower water and season to taste with salt and pepper. Cover and cook for a further 5 minutes, or until the duck is tender.

In a skillet, melt the butter and stir in the almonds. Sauté until golden brown and then scatter them over the duck. Serve immediately with Plain, Buttery Couscous tossed with preserved lemon and green herbs.

duck tagine with pears and cinnamon

This traditional tagine can be prepared with duck, chicken, Cornish game hens, or quails. Variations of the recipe can include quince, plums, apples, cherries, and apricots. Serve with bread to mop up the syrupy juices or with Plain, Buttery Couscous.

• •

2 tablespoons olive oil plus
a pat of butter

2 onions, finely chopped

a 1-inch piece of fresh ginger, peeled
and finely chopped

2 cinnamon sticks

a pinch of saffron threads

2 lbs. duck meat, from the thigh,
breast or leg, off the bone and
cut into bite-size pieces

2 tablespoons butter

3–4 tablespoons clear, runny honey

3 pears, peeled, quartered and cored

2–3 tablespoons orange flower water

sea salt and freshly ground
black pepper

1–2 tablespoons toasted sesame seeds

a few lemon balm leaves, to garnish
(optional)

crusty bread or Plain, Buttery
Couscous (see page 108), to serve

Serves 4–6

Heat the oil and butter in a tagine or heavy-based saucepan. Add the onions and ginger and sauté until they begin to color, then add the cinnamon sticks and saffron. Toss in the duck, making sure it is well coated in the ginger and onions. Pour in 2 cups water and bring it to a boil. Reduce the heat, cover and simmer gently for about 40 minutes, until the duck is tender.

Meanwhile, melt the butter in a heavy-based saucepan and stir in the honey. Toss in the pears and cook gently until they begin to caramelize. Add the pears to the duck with the orange flower water and cook the tagine for a further 10 minutes.

Season to taste with salt and pepper and scatter the roasted sesame seeds over the top. Garnish with the lemon balm leaves, if using, and serve with crusty bread or Plain, Buttery Couscous.

fish and seafood tagines

fish tagine with preserved lemon and mint

The fish tagines of coastal Morocco are often made with whole fish, or with large chunks of fleshy fish such as sea bass, monkfish, and cod. The fish is first marinated in a chermoula-style flavoring, and the dish is given an additional fillip with a little white wine or sherry. Serve with new potatoes and leafy salad greens.

• •

2 lbs. fresh fish fillets, such as cod or haddock, cut into large chunks

2–3 tablespoons olive oil

1 red onion, finely chopped

2 carrots, finely chopped

2 celery ribs, finely chopped

1 preserved lemon (see page 11), finely chopped

14-oz. can plum tomatoes with their juice

⅔ cup fish stock or water

⅔ cup white wine or fino sherry

sea salt and freshly ground black pepper

leaves from a bunch of fresh mint, finely shredded

For the chermoula:

2–3 garlic cloves, chopped

1 red chile, seeded and chopped

1 teaspoon sea salt

a small bunch of cilantro

a pinch of saffron threads

1–2 teaspoons ground cumin

3–4 tablespoons olive oil

freshly squeezed juice of 1 lemon

Serves 4–6

First, make the chermoula. Using a mortar and pestle, pound the garlic and chile with the salt to form a paste. Add the cilantro and pound to a coarse paste. Beat in the saffron threads and cumin and bind well with the olive oil and lemon juice (you can whizz all the ingredients together in an electric blender, if you prefer.) Reserve 2 teaspoons of the mixture for cooking. Toss the fish chunks in the remaining chermoula, cover and leave to marinate in the refrigerator for 1–2 hours.

Heat the oil in a tagine or heavy-based casserole dish. Stir in the onion, carrots, and celery and sauté until softened. Add the preserved lemon (reserving a little for sprinkling) with the reserved 2 teaspoons of chermoula and the tomatoes and stir in well. Cook gently for about 10 minutes to reduce the liquid, then add the stock and the wine or sherry. Bring the liquid to a boil, cover the tagine, reduce the heat and simmer for 10–15 minutes.

Toss the fish in the tagine, cover and cook gently for 6–8 minutes, until the fish is cooked through. Season to taste with salt and pepper, sprinkle with the reserved preserved lemon and the shredded mint leaves and serve immediately.

tagine of monkfish, potatoes, cherry tomatoes, and black olives

For this lovely tagine, flavored with garlic, chile, cumin, and cilantro (a popular version of Morocco's favorite chermoula spice mix), you can used any meaty white fish. Serve it as a meal in itself with chunks of fresh, crusty bread to mop up the delicious juices, or with Plain, Buttery Couscous.

* *

1 quantity Chermoula (see page 12)

2 lbs. monkfish tail, cut into chunks

12 small new potatoes

3 tablespoons olive oil plus a pat of butter

3–4 garlic cloves, thinly sliced

12–16 cherry tomatoes

2 green bell peppers, broiled until black, skinned, and cut into strips

sea salt and freshly ground black pepper

12 black olives

1 lemon, cut into wedges, to serve

crusty bread or Plain, Buttery Couscous (see page 108), to serve

Serves 4-6

First, make the chermoula. Put the fish in a shallow dish and rub it with most of the chermoula (reserve a little for cooking). Cover and leave to marinate in the refrigerator for 1–2 hours.

Meanwhile, bring a saucepan of water to a boil and add the potatoes. Boil vigorously for about 8 minutes to soften them a little, then drain and refresh under cold running water. Peel and cut in half lengthwise.

Heat 2 tablespoons of the olive oil with the butter in a tagine or heavy-based saucepan. Stir in the garlic and, when it begins to brown, add the tomatoes to soften them. Add the skinned bell peppers and the reserved chermoula, and season to taste with salt and pepper. Tip the mixture onto a plate.

Arrange the potatoes over the base of the tagine and spoon half of the tomato and pepper mixture over them. Place the chunks of marinated fish on top and spoon the rest of the tomato and pepper mixture over the fish. Tuck the olives in and around the fish and drizzle the remaining tablespoon of olive oil over the top. Pour in ½ cup water, cover with a lid, and steam for 15–20 minutes, until the fish is cooked through. Serve immediately with wedges of lemon.

saffron sea bass tagine with potatoes and bell peppers

This is one of the traditional oven-baked tagines, which are incredibly simple and satisfying. Versatile in nature, this dish can be altered to accommodate any selection of vegetables, such as leeks, zucchini, Swiss chard, fava beans, and fennel.

• •

a pinch of saffron threads

⅔ cups warm water

2 lbs. new potatoes, peeled and sliced

4 large tomatoes, sliced (reserve a few slices to top the fish)

4–6 garlic cloves, peeled and smashed

2 green bell peppers, seeded and cut into long strips (reserve a few strips to top the fish)

4 tablespoons olive oil

freshly squeezed juice of 2 lemons

1 sea bass (roughly 2 lbs. 12 oz.), gutted and thoroughly cleaned

the rind of a small preserved lemon, or half a large one, cut into fine strips (see page 11)

2 tablespoons green olives, pitted and sliced

a small bunch of cilantro, chopped

sea salt and freshly ground black pepper

Serves 4–6

Preheat the oven to 350°F.

First prepare the saffron. Dry roast the threads in a small heavy-based skillet for less than 1 minute, until they emit a faint aroma. Using a mortar and pestle, grind them to a powder and stir in the water until the saffron dissolves.

Line the base of an oven tagine, or an ovenproof dish, with a layer of potatoes, topped with a layer of sliced tomatoes. Scatter the garlic over the top, season with a little salt and pepper and arrange the bell peppers over the top. Pour half the prepared saffron, half the olive oil, and half the lemon juice over the layers, cover and place it in the preheated oven for about 25 minutes, until the potatoes and bell peppers are tender.

Rub the sea bass with a little salt and place it on top of the peppers. Mark the topside of the fish with 2–3 gashes and pour the rest of the prepared saffron, olive oil, and lemon juice over it. Arrange the reserved tomato and bell pepper slices over the top and scatter the preserved lemon and olives over and around the fish. Cover the tagine and return to the oven for another 25 minutes, until the fish is just cooked. Remove the lid and return the fish to the oven for a final 10 minutes. Scatter the cilantro over the top and serve with crusty bread or Plain, Buttery Couscous.

oven-baked tagine of red mullet, tomatoes, and lime

Baking whole fish in a tagine keeps the flesh deliciously moist. Obviously, you need to select fish that fits snugly into your tagine or ovenproof dish. The most popular fish for oven-baking in North Africa include red mullet, sardines, red snapper, grouper, and sea bass. You could serve this dish with Plain, Buttery Couscous or a tangy salad.

• •

2 tablespoons olive oil

2 tablespoons butter

2–3 garlic cloves, thinly sliced

3–4 good-size red mullet, gutted and cleaned

sea salt

2–3 large tomatoes, thinly sliced

1 lime, thinly sliced

To serve:

leaves from a small bunch of fresh flat-leaf parsley, coarsely chopped

1 lime, cut into wedges

Serves 3–4

Preheat the oven to 350°F.

Heat the olive oil and butter in an oven tagine or ovenproof dish. Add the garlic and sauté, stirring, until it begins to brown. Put the fish in the tagine and cook it until the skin has browned and lightly buckled. (If you are using an ovenproof dish, brown the garlic and fish in a large skillet first.)

Turn off the heat, sprinkle a little salt over the fish, and tuck the slices of tomato and lime over and around them. Cover and cook in the preheated oven for about 15 minutes.

Uncover and bake for a further 5–10 minutes, until the fish is cooked and nicely browned on top (you could do this under the broiler, if you prefer.)

Sprinkle the parsley over the top and serve with wedges of lime to squeeze over the fish.

shrimp tagine with saffron, ginger, and fennel

Many shellfish tagines are not so much traditional as they are inspired by cultural influences, such as the shrimp and mussel tagines of Tangier that resemble the cooking of Andalusia across the water. You can serve this delicious tagine as an appetizer or entrée with chunks of crusty bread.

● ●

4–5 tablespoons olive oil

20 raw jumbo shrimp, heads removed

2 onions, finely chopped

2 garlic cloves, finely chopped

1-inch piece of fresh ginger, peeled and finely chopped

a pinch of saffron threads

1–2 teaspoons smoked paprika

14-oz. can tomatoes, drained of juice

leaves from a small bunch of cilantro, finely chopped

leaves from a small bunch of fresh flat-leaf parsley, finely chopped

1 teaspoon sugar

4 fennel bulbs, trimmed and sliced thickly lengthwise

sea salt and freshly ground black pepper

crusty bread, to serve

Serves 4-6

Heat 2–3 tablespoons of the olive oil in the base of a tagine or heavy-based casserole dish. Add the shrimp and cook for 2–3 minutes, until they turn opaque. Using a slotted spoon, remove the shrimp from the tagine and set aside. Keep the oil in the pan.

Stir the onion, garlic, ginger, and saffron into the oil and sauté for 3–4 minutes, until they begin to color. Add the paprika, tomatoes, and half the herbs. Stir in the sugar and season with salt and pepper. Cook gently, partially covered, for about 10 minutes until the mixture thickens to form a sauce.

Meanwhile, steam the fennel for about 5 minutes, until it softens. Heat the remaining olive oil in a skillet and add the steamed fennel. Cook gently on both sides for 4–5 minutes, until it turns golden. Sprinkle with salt and pepper.

Toss the cooked shrimp in the tomato sauce, place the fennel on top, cover, and cook gently for 5 minutes. Sprinkle with the remaining cilantro and parsley immediately before serving.

creamy shellfish tagine with fennel and harissa

In some coastal areas of Morocco, such as Casablanca and Tangier, restaurants offer shellfish tagines—a modern speciality, rather than a traditional one. Whether these dishes are the result of colonial French influence or simply devised for the tourists, they are certainly very tasty. They are best appreciated on their own, with chunks of crusty bread to mop up the creamy sauce.

* *

1 lb. fresh mussels in their shells, scrubbed clean and rinsed

1 lb. raw shrimp in their shells, thoroughly rinsed

freshly squeezed juice of 1 lemon

2 tablespoons olive oil

4–6 shallots, finely chopped

1 fennel bulb, chopped

1–2 teaspoons harissa paste (see page 12)

⅔ cup heavy cream

sea salt and freshly ground black pepper

leaves from a large bunch of cilantro, finely chopped

crusty bread, to serve

Serves 4–6

Put the mussels and shrimp in a large saucepan with just enough water to cover them. Add the lemon juice, cover the pan, and bring the liquid to a boil. Shake the pan and cook the shellfish for about 3 minutes, until the shells of the mussels have opened. Drain the shellfish, reserve the liquor, and discard any mussels that have not opened. Refresh the mussels and shrimp under cold running water and shell most of them (you can, of course, leave them all in their shells if you prefer, as long as you are prepared for messy eating.)

Heat the olive oil in a tagine or heavy-based casserole dish. Add the shallots and fennel and sauté, stirring, until soft. Stir in the harissa and pour in 1¼ cups of the reserved cooking liquor. Bring the liquid to a boil and continue to boil for 2–3 minutes, reduce the heat and stir in the cream. Simmer gently for about 5 minutes to let the flavors mingle, season to taste with salt and plenty of black pepper, and stir in the mussels and shrimp. Toss in half the cilantro, cover, and cook gently for about 5 minutes.

Sprinkle the remaining cilantro over the top and serve immediately with crusty bread.

vegetable tagines

tagine of butternut squash, shallots, golden raisins, and almonds

Substantial enough for an entrée, served with Plain, Buttery Couscous and yogurt, vegetable tagines also make good sides for grilled or roasted meats or meat tagines. You can cook this recipe in the oven if you like, using the tagine base or an ovenproof dish.

• •

3 tablespoons olive oil plus
a pat of butter

12 shallots, peeled and left whole

8 garlic cloves, lightly crushed

⅔ cup golden raisins

⅔ cup blanched almonds

1–2 teaspoons harissa paste
(see page 12)

2 tablespoons dark, runny honey

1 medium butternut squash,
halved lengthwise, peeled,
seeded, and sliced

sea salt and freshly ground
black pepper

leaves from a small bunch of cilantro,
finely chopped

lemon wedges, to serve

Plain, Buttery Couscous (see page
108), to serve (optional)

Serves 3–4

Heat the oil and butter in a tagine or heavy-based casserole dish. Add the shallots and garlic and sauté, stirring, until they begin to color. Add the golden raisins and almonds and stir in the harissa and honey. Toss in the squash, making sure it is coated in the oil.

Pour in enough water to cover the base of the tagine and cover. Cook gently for 15–20 minutes, until the shallots and squash are tender but still quite firm.

Season to taste with salt and pepper, sprinkle the cilantro leaves over the top, and serve with wedges of lemon to squeeze over the dish and Plain, Buttery Couscous, if liked.

tagine of artichokes, potatoes, peas, and saffron

You can make this hearty country dish with either fresh or frozen artichokes. If using fresh, you must first remove the outer leaves, then cut off the stems and scoop out the choke and hairy bits with a teaspoon. Rub the artichokes with lemon juice or place in a bowl of ice water with lemon juice to prevent discoloration.

• •

2–3 tablespoons olive oil

2 red onions, halved lengthwise, cut in half crosswise, and sliced with the grain

4 garlic cloves, crushed

2 teaspoons coriander seeds

1 teaspoon cumin seeds

2 teaspoons ground turmeric

1–2 teaspoons dried mint

8 medium waxy potatoes, peeled and quartered

1½ cups vegetable or chicken stock

4 prepared artichokes, quartered

leaves from a small bunch of cilantro, chopped

1½ cups fresh or frozen peas

½ preserved lemon (see page 11), finely shredded

sea salt and freshly ground black pepper

leaves from a small bunch of fresh mint, to serve

crusty bread or Plain, Buttery Couscous (see page 108), to serve

Serves 4–6

Heat the olive oil in a tagine or heavy-based casserole dish. Add the onion and sauté, stirring, until it begins to soften. Add the garlic, coriander and cumin seeds, ground turmeric, and the dried mint. Toss in the potatoes, coating them in the spices. Pour in the stock and bring to a boil. Reduce the heat, cover, and cook gently for about 10 minutes.

Toss in the artichokes and cilantro and cook for a further 5 minutes. Stir in the peas and preserved lemon, and season to taste with salt and pepper. Cook gently for 5–10 minutes, uncovered, until the artichokes are tender and the liquid has reduced.

Sprinkle with the fresh mint leaves and serve with crusty bread or Plain, Buttery Couscous.

tagine of yam, shallots, carrots, and prunes

This syrupy, caramelized tagine is delicious served as a main dish, with Plain, Buttery Couscous and a herby salad, or as a side to accompany grilled or roasted meats. Sweet potatoes, butternut squash, and pumpkin can be used instead of yam, if you prefer.

◆ ◆

2–3 tablespoons olive oil plus
a pat of butter

1½ inch piece of fresh ginger, peeled
and finely chopped or grated

1–2 cinnamon sticks or 1–2 teaspoons
ground cinnamon

16 small shallots, peeled and
left whole

1¾ lbs. yam, peeled and cut into
bite-size pieces

2 carrots, peeled and cut into
bite-size pieces

¾ cup ready-to-eat pitted prunes

1 tablespoon dark, runny honey

1¾ cups vegetable or chicken stock

leaves from a small bunch of cilantro,
roughly chopped

a few fresh mint leaves, chopped

sea salt and freshly ground
black pepper

Plain, Buttery Couscous (see page
108), to serve (optional)

Serves 4–6

Heat the olive oil and butter in a tagine or heavy-based casserole dish. Add the ginger and cinnamon sticks. Toss in the shallots and when they begin to color add the yam and the carrots. Sauté for 2–3 minutes, stirring, then add the prunes and the honey. Pour in the stock and bring it to a boil. Reduce the heat, cover, and cook gently for about 25 minutes.

Uncover and stir in some of the cilantro and mint. Season to taste with salt and pepper and reduce the liquid, if necessary, by cooking for a further 2–3 minutes uncovered. The vegetables should be tender and slightly caramelized in a very syrupy sauce.

Sprinkle with the remaining cilantro and mint and serve immediately with Plain, Buttery Couscous, if liked.

tagine of butter beans, cherry tomatoes, and black olives

As butter beans are so meaty, this tagine makes a substantial entrée, but it is also excellent as an accompaniment to grilled or roasted meats and poultry. Bean dishes like this vary from region to region in Morocco, sometimes spiked with chiles or hot merguez, chorizo-style sausages.

* *

1 cup dried butter beans, soaked overnight in plenty of water

2–3 tablespoons olive oil plus a pat of butter

4 garlic cloves, halved and crushed

2 red onions, halved lengthwise, cut in half crosswise, and sliced with the grain

1–2 red or green chiles, seeded and thinly sliced

1–2 teaspoons coriander seeds, crushed

a 1-inch piece of fresh ginger, peeled and finely shredded or chopped

a pinch of saffron threads

16–20 cherry tomatoes

1–2 teaspoons sugar

1–2 teaspoons dried thyme

2–3 tablespoons black olives, pitted

freshly squeezed juice of 1 lemon

sea salt and freshly ground black pepper

leaves from a small bunch of flat-leaf parsley, coarsely chopped

crusty bread and plain yogurt, to serve (optional)

Serves 4–6

Drain and rinse the soaked beans. Put them in a deep saucepan with plenty of water and bring to a boil. Boil for 5 minutes, then reduce the heat and simmer gently for about 1 hour, or until the beans are tender but not mushy. Drain and refresh under cold running water.

Heat the olive oil and butter in a tagine or heavy-based casserole dish. Add the garlic, onions, and chiles and sauté, stirring, until they soften. Add the coriander seeds, ginger, and saffron. Cover and cook gently for 4–5 minutes. Toss in the tomatoes with the sugar and thyme, cover with the lid again, and cook until the skin on the tomatoes begins to crinkle.

Toss in the beans and olives, pour over the lemon juice, and season to taste with salt and pepper. Cover and cook gently for about 5 minutes, until the beans and olives are heated through. Sprinkle with the flat-leaf parsley and serve with crusty bread and a dollop of thick, creamy plain yogurt, if liked.

tagine of baby eggplants with cilantro and mint

This vegetarian tagine is best made with baby eggplants, but you can also use slender, larger eggplants cut into quarters lengthwise. As an entrée, it is delicious served with Plain, Buttery Couscous and a dollop of thick, creamy yogurt; it can also be served as a side to accompany meat or poultry.

◆ ◆

1–2 tablespoons olive oil

1 tablespoon butter or ghee

1–2 red onions, halved lengthwise and sliced with the grain

3–4 garlic cloves, crushed

1–2 red chiles, seeded and sliced, or 2–3 dried red chiles, left whole

1–2 teaspoons coriander seeds, roasted and crushed

1–2 teaspoons cumin seeds, roasted and crushed

2 teaspoons sugar

16 baby eggplants, with stalks intact

2 x 14-oz. cans chopped tomatoes

sea salt and freshly ground black pepper

leaves from a bunch of fresh mint, roughly chopped

leaves from a bunch of cilantro, roughly chopped

Plain, Buttery Couscous (see page 108) and plain yogurt, to serve (optional)

Serves 4

Heat the oil and butter in a tagine or heavy-based casserole dish. Add the onions and garlic and sauté, stirring, until they begin to color. Add the chiles, the coriander and cumin seeds, and the sugar. When the seeds give off a nutty aroma, toss in the whole baby eggplants, coating them in the onion and spices. Tip in the tomatoes, cover, and cook gently for about 40 minutes, until the eggplants are beautifully tender.

Season to taste with salt and pepper and add half the mint and cilantro leaves. Cover and simmer for a further 5–10 minutes.

Sprinkle with the remaining mint and cilantro leaves and serve hot with Plain, Buttery Couscous and a dollop of thick, creamy plain yogurt, if liked.

spicy carrot and chickpea tagine with turmeric and cilantro

This country-style dish is vegetarian, typical of regions where meat is regarded as a luxury by most families. Legumes of all kinds and, in particular, chickpeas, provide the nourishing content of these dishes. To avoid lengthy preparation and cooking, use canned chickpeas. For simple accompaniments, offer natural yogurt and bread.

• •

3–4 tablespoons olive oil

1 onion, finely chopped

3–4 garlic cloves, finely chopped

2 teaspoons ground turmeric

1–2 teaspoons cumin seeds

1 teaspoon ground cinnamon

½ teaspoon cayenne pepper

½ teaspoon ground black pepper

1 tablespoon dark, runny honey

3–4 carrots, sliced on the diagonal

2 x 14-oz. cans chickpeas, rinsed and drained

sea salt

1–2 tablespoons rosewater

leaves from a bunch of cilantro, finely chopped

lemon wedges, to serve

crusty bread and plain yogurt, to serve (optional)

Serves 4

Heat the oil in a tagine or heavy-based casserole dish. Add the onion and garlic and sauté, stirring, until soft. Add the turmeric, cumin seeds, cinnamon, cayenne pepper, black pepper, honey, and carrots. Pour in enough water to cover the base of the tagine and cover. Cook gently for about 10–15 minutes.

Toss in the chickpeas, check that there is still enough liquid at the base of the tagine, adding a little more water if necessary. Cover and cook gently for a further 5–10 minutes until all the vegetables are tender.

Season with salt, sprinkle the rosewater and cilantro leaves over the top and arrange the lemon wedges on the side. Serve with crusty bread and a dollop of thick, creamy plain yogurt, if liked.

baked vegetable tagine with preserved lemon

This vegetable tagine can be served as a side or on its own with Plain, Buttery Couscous or flat bread to dip into it. Vegetable tagines vary with the seasons and can be prepared on the stovetop or in the oven. For the baked version, you need a traditional Berber tagine with a domed lid, rather than the steep conical one, or you can use an earthenware baking dish, covered with foil.

* *

2–3 tablespoons olive oil

2 onions, halved and sliced with the grain

4 garlic cloves, chopped

a thumb-size piece of fresh ginger, peeled and chopped

1–2 red chiles, seeded and chopped

1 teaspoon cumin seeds

1 teaspoon paprika

3–4 good-size potatoes, peeled and thickly sliced

2 good-size carrots, peeled and thickly sliced

8–10 broccoli florets

2½ cups vegetable or chicken stock

2 cups fresh or frozen peas

1 preserved lemon (see page 11), thickly sliced

leaves from a bunch of cilantro, coarsely chopped

sea salt and freshly ground black pepper

4–6 large tomatoes, sliced

2 tablespoons butter

crusty bread or Plain, Buttery Couscous (see page 108), to serve

Serves 4

Preheat the oven to 350°F.

Heat the oil in a tagine or heavy-based casserole dish. Add the onions and sauté until they begin to color. Add the garlic, ginger, and chiles and cook for 1–2 minutes. Stir in the cumin seeds and paprika then toss in the potatoes, carrots, and broccoli. Pour in the stock, cover, and place the tagine in the oven for about 20 minutes, until the potatoes, carrots, and broccoli are tender but still firm and most of the liquid has reduced.

Season with salt and pepper. Toss in the peas, preserved lemon, and half the cilantro. Arrange the tomato slices, overlapping each other, on top and dot them with little pieces of butter. Pop the tagine back into the oven, uncovered, to brown the top of the tomatoes.

Garnish with the remaining cilantro and serve from the tagine with Plain, Buttery Couscous or crusty bread.

three pepper tagine with eggs

This is one of those dishes you'll find in Morocco at street stalls, bus stations and working men's cafes. Quick, easy and colorful, it is a great dish for lunch or a tasty snack, served with warmed flat breads.

* *

2 tablespoons olive oil or ghee

1 onion, halved lengthwise and sliced

2–3 garlic cloves, chopped

1–2 teaspoons coriander seeds

1 teaspoon cumin seeds

3 bell peppers (green, red, and yellow), seeded and cut into slices

2 tablespoons green olives, pitted and finely sliced

sea salt and freshly ground black pepper

4–6 very fresh eggs

1 teaspoon paprika or dried hot pepper flakes

leaves from a small bunch of flat-leaf parsley, coarsely chopped

warmed flat breads, to serve

Serves 4–6

Heat the oil in the base of a tagine, flameproof baking dish, or heavy-based skillet. Add the onions, garlic, cumin and coriander seeds, and sauté, stirring, until the onions begin to soften. Toss in the bell peppers and olives and sauté until they begin to color. Season well with salt and pepper.

Using your spoon, push aside the peppers to form little pockets for the eggs. Crack the eggs in the pockets and cover for 4–5 minutes until the eggs are cooked. Scatter the paprika over the top and sprinkle with the parsley.

Serve immediately from the tagine or pan, with warmed flat bread on the side.

couscous
dishes

the art of making couscous

Couscous is Morocco's national dish. It is prepared throughout the country and is a traditional staple of the whole of the North African region, right down to Senegal and across to Chad. Further east in Egypt and parts of the Middle East, it is known as *moghrabiyyeh*, "the dish of the North Africans." Although referred to as a "grain", couscous is not technically one; instead it could be more accurately described as Moroccan "pasta" as it is made with semolina flour and water and then hand-rolled and dried even though it is prepared and served like rice.

Couscous is of fundamental value to Moroccan culture for dietary, religious, and symbolic reasons, as Moroccans believe it is a food that brings God's blessing upon those who consume it. It is therefore prepared in every household on Muslim holy days and on Fridays, the Islamic day of rest, when it is

traditionally distributed to the poor as well. At festive and religious feasts, such as the traditional *diffas* to celebrate births and weddings, or the Berber *moussems*, a mound of couscous is served as the magnificent crown to end the meal. There is a Moroccan saying that "each granule of couscous represents a good deed" so it is not surprising that thousands of granules are consumed in a day.

There are many different types of couscous in Morocco, some made with wheat flour, others with barley, maize, or millet. In the rural areas, the village women still buy sacks of wheat, which they take to the local mill to be ground to semolina, and then laboriously prepare couscous every week by sprinkling the semolina flour with water and raking it with their fingers in a circular motion to form tiny balls. The balls are then rubbed against the side of the bowl using the palm of the hand and passed through a fine strainer to form a uniform size: *kesksou* is ⅛ inch in diameter; *seffa* or *mefuf* is ultra-fine at 1/16 inch in diameter and is mainly reserved for fillings and sweet dishes; and *mhammsa* is ⅛ inch in diameter. The tiny granules are then spread out to dry before use. In modern households in the cities, many cooks prefer to buy sacks of ready-prepared couscous which needs to be steamed several times before eating. Outside Morocco, the most commonly available packages of couscous have been taken one step further as they are already precooked and only require soaking in water to swell, before being fluffed up aerated using fingers and olive oil. The recipes in this book use this precooked version, which is available in larger stores.

The preparation of couscous varies from region to region and is dependent on the type of granules, but the principal method involves placing the dried granules in a *ga'saa*—a wide, flat earthenware dish—and sprinkling them liberally with water. The moistened granules are then transferred to the metal *keskess*, a colander, and set snugly atop a *q'draa*, a large tin-lined, copper pot, which contains water or a stew of meat or vegetables. The utensils together are known in French as the two-tiered pot, the *couscoussière*, and this is the name that is used in international culinary circles. The steam between the *keskess* and the *q'draa* is sealed with a piece of cloth which is dipped in a mixture of flour and water. The couscous is then steamed, uncovered, until puffs of vapour emanate from the granules. The warm couscous is then returned to the *ga'saa* and mixed with more water before being returned to the

colander and steamed a second time until the granules become soft and plump. Finally it is flavored with lashings of butter, olive oil, or smen (see page 11), which is rubbed into the grains with the fingertips, and it is moistened with the broth from the stew. This preparation plays such an important role in the culinary life of most Moroccans that it determines a cook's ability—the granules should be light and airy, almost floating above the plate and heavenly to touch and taste.

To the majority of Moroccans a meal would be unthinkable without couscous. It is extremely versatile and is traditionally served as a course on its own, but it can also be served as an accompaniment to tagines or grilled and roasted meats. It can look truly spectacular, particularly when piled high in a cone-shaped mound for banquets and topped with stuffed pigeons, dates, and almonds, or decorated with strips of colorful vegetables and topped with sweet onions and raisins tinged yellow with saffron and it is often accompanied by little side dishes, such as spicy chickpeas, marinated raisins, and harissa paste (see page 12.) Eating couscous in a traditional manner is an experience in itself and requires a little practice. It is a communal dish so, once the mound has been set on the ground, or on a low table, diners literally ram their right hands, palm upwards, into the grains to extract a handful and then, using the thumb and first two fingers, deftly roll the grains to form small tight balls that might incorporate some small pieces of meat or vegetables, and flip them into their mouths. It looks easy but, on first attempts, the sauce dribbles down your wrist and the granules spill all over the table!

plain, buttery couscous

Traditionally, plain, buttery couscous, piled high in a mound, is served as a dish on its own after a tagine or roasted meat. It is held in such high esteem that religious feasts and celebratory meals would be unthinkable with it. The par-boiled couscous available outside Morocco is extremely easy to prepare, making it a practical accompaniment for many dishes featured in this book.

◆ ◆

2 cups couscous, rinsed and drained

½ teaspoon sea salt

1⅔ cups warm water

2 tablespoons olive or sunflower oil

2 tablespoons butter, broken into little pieces

For the top:

1 tablespoon butter

2–3 tablespoons blanched, slivered almonds

Serves 4–6

Preheat the oven to 350°F.

Tip the couscous into an ovenproof dish. Stir the salt into the water and pour it over the couscous. Leave the couscous to absorb the water for about 10 minutes.

Using your fingers, rub the oil into the couscous grains to break up the lumps and aerate them. Scatter the butter over the surface and cover with a piece of foil or wet parchment paper. Put in the preheated oven for about 15 minutes, until the couscous is heated through.

Meanwhile, prepare the almonds. Melt the butter in a heavy-based skillet set over medium heat, add the almonds and cook, stirring until they begin to turn golden. Remove from the pan and drain on paper towels.

Take the couscous out of the oven and fluff up the grains with a fork. Serve it from the dish or tip it onto a plate and pile it high in a mound, with the toasted almonds scattered over the top.

green couscous with a spring broth

This is a lovely spring or summer couscous dish as it is prepared with the young green vegetables in season, such as fresh fava beans and peas, artichokes, asparagus, arugula leaves, scallions, and baby zucchini.

• •

3 cups couscous

½ teaspoon sea salt

2¾ cups warm water

1–2 tablespoons olive oil

1 tablespoon butter, broken into small pieces

4 cups vegetable or chicken stock

12 oz. fresh fava beans, shelled

6 oz. fresh or frozen peas

12 scallions, trimmed and thickly sliced

6 baby zucchini, thickly sliced

4–6 globe artichoke hearts, cut into quarters

leaves from a bunch of fresh flat-leaf parsley, finely chopped

leaves from a bunch of cilantro, finely chopped

leaves from a bunch of fresh mint, finely chopped

sea salt and freshly ground black pepper

Serves 4–6

Preheat the oven to 400°F.

Tip the couscous into an ovenproof dish. Stir the salt into the water and pour it over the couscous. Leave the couscous to absorb the water for about 10 minutes.

Using your fingers, rub the oil into the couscous grains to break up the lumps and aerate them. Scatter the butter over the surface and cover with a piece of foil or wet parchment paper. Put in the preheated oven for about 15 minutes, until the couscous is heated through.

Meanwhile, prepare the vegetable broth. Pour the stock into a heavy-based saucepan and bring it to a boil. Add the fava beans, peas, scallions, zucchini, and artichokes and cook for 5–10 minutes, until tender. Season the broth to taste with salt and pepper and stir in the herbs.

Remove the couscous from the oven and tip it onto a serving plate. Using a slotted spoon, lift the vegetables out of the broth and arrange them around, or over, the mound of couscous. Moisten with a little of the broth, then pour the rest into a small pitcher and serve separately to pour over the couscous.

lemon couscous with roasted vegetables

This is a modern recipe and ideal for vegetarians. For a variation, instead of roasting the vegetables, you could prepare vegetable kabobs on the grill and serve them with the couscous. Generally, eggplants, zucchini, and bell peppers are roasted together but you can vary the vegetables, according to the season.

◆ ◆

8 baby eggplants, left whole

3–4 small zucchini, cut into 4 lengthwise

2 red bell peppers, seeded and cut into 4 lengthwise

4 garlic cloves, peeled and cut into 4 lengthwise

a thumb-size piece of fresh ginger, peeled and cut into thin sticks

6 tablespoons olive oil

sea salt

leaves from a bunch of cilantro, coarsely chopped

leaves from a bunch of fresh mint, coarsely chopped

For the Lemon Couscous:

3 cups couscous

½ teaspoon sea salt

2¾ cups warm water

1–2 tablespoons olive oil

1 preserved lemon (see page 11), finely chopped

1 tablespoon butter, broken into small pieces

Serves 4

Preheat the oven to 400°F.

Put the vegetables, garlic, and ginger in an ovenproof dish. Pour over the oil, sprinkle with salt and cook in the preheated oven for about 40 minutes, until the vegetables are tender and nicely browned.

To make the lemon couscous, tip the couscous into an ovenproof dish. Stir the salt into the water and pour it over the couscous. Leave it to absorb the water for about 10 minutes.

Using your fingers, rub the oil into the couscous grains to break up the lumps and aerate them. Toss in the preserved lemon, scatter the butter over the surface and cover with a piece of foil or wet parchment paper. Put the dish in the oven for about 15 minutes, until the couscous has heated through.

Tip the couscous onto a serving plate in a mound. Arrange the vegetables over and around it and spoon some of the roasting oil over the top. Sprinkle with the cilantro and mint and serve immediately.

fish and shellfish k'dra with couscous

In the coastal regions, this is the king of fish dishes. Prepared in vast quantities for a family celebration, it combines the riches of the sea and the land in one big copper pot. Any firm-fleshed fish such as haddock, halibut, or sea bass will work here.

* *

2 tablespoons olive oil

2 teaspoons cumin seeds

2 teaspoons coriander seeds

2 teaspoons ground turmeric

1 tablespoon harissa paste
(see page 12)

leaves from a small bunch of
flat-leaf parsley, finely chopped

2 quarts fish stock or water

4–6 garlic cloves, finely sliced

2 x 14-oz. cans whole plum tomatoes

2–3 carrots, cut into matchsticks

2–3 zucchini, cut into matchsticks

2 lbs. firm-fleshed fish fillets

1 lb. raw shrimp, shelled and deveined

1 lb. fresh mussels, cleaned

1 lb. scallops, shelled and cleaned

leaves from a small bunch of cilantro,
finely chopped

sea salt and freshly ground
black pepper

For the couscous:

3 cups couscous, rinsed and drained

2¾ cups warm water

2 tablespoons olive or sunflower oil

2 tablespoons butter, broken into
little pieces

Serves 4–6

Preheat the oven to 350°F.

Tip the couscous grains into an ovenproof dish. Stir ½ teaspoon salt into the water and pour it over the couscous. Set aside for about 20 minutes.

Meanwhile, heat the oil in a large copper pot, or very large heavy-based saucepan. Stir in the cumin and coriander seeds, turmeric, and harissa paste. Add the parsley and pour in the fish stock. Bring the liquid to a boil, reduce the heat, and simmer for 5 minutes. Add the garlic, drained tomatoes, carrots, and zucchini and simmer for a further 10 minutes.

Using your fingers, rub the oil into the couscous grains to break up the lumps and aerate them. Scatter the butter over the top and cover with a piece of foil or wet parchment paper. Place in the oven for about 15 minutes to heat through.

Add the fish and shellfish to the simmering broth and cook for 5–10 minutes, until the fish is flaky, the shrimp opaque, and the shells of the mussels have opened (discard any that remain closed.) Season to taste with salt and pepper and stir in a little cilantro.

Fluff up the couscous with a fork and pile it onto a large serving plate in a domed mound. Spoon the fish and shellfish around the couscous and drizzle with a little of the broth. Ladle the rest of the broth into individual bowls and serve immediately.

couscous tfaia with beef

This dish would traditionally be made in a *couscoussière* (see page 107) with the meat cooking in the bottom compartment creating the steam for the couscous above. However, the couscous can be prepared separately and the dish combined at the end. The tfaia is a sweet mixture of onions and raisins that is spooned on top of the stew.

• •

1½ lbs. beef rump or chuck, cut into bite-size pieces

1 onion, chopped

1 teaspoon ground coriander

1 teaspoon ground cumin

a pinch of saffron threads

3 cups couscous

2¾ cups warm water

1–2 tablespoons olive oil

1 tablespoon butter, broken

For the tfaia:

1–2 tablespoons olive oil

2 tablespoons butter

4 onions, thinly sliced

1–2 teaspoons cinnamon

1 teaspoon ground ginger

1 teaspoon saffron threads, soaked in 2 tablespoons warm water

2 tablespoons runny honey

3 tablespoons golden raisins, soaked in warm water for 15 minutes and drained

sea salt and freshly ground black pepper

Serves 4–6

Preheat the oven to 350°F.

Put the beef in the base of a tagine or heavy-based casserole dish with the onion, spices, and saffron. Pour in just enough water to cover, then bring to a boil. Reduce the heat, cover and simmer for about 1 hour.

Meanwhile, tip the couscous into an ovenproof dish. Stir ½ teaspoon salt into the water and pour it over the couscous. Leave the couscous to absorb the water for about 10 minutes. Using your fingers, rub the oil into the couscous grains to break up the lumps and aerate them. Scatter the butter over the top and cover with a piece of foil or wet parchment paper. Put the dish in the preheated oven for about 15 minutes, until the couscous is heated through.

To prepare the tfaia, heat the oil and butter in a heavy-based saucepan. Add the onions and sauté for 1–2 minutes, until softened. Reduce the heat and add the spices, saffron water, and honey and season to taste with salt and pepper. Cover and cook gently for 15–20 minutes. Stir in the golden raisins and cook, uncovered, for a further 10 minutes.

Tip the couscous onto a serving dish and create a well in the center. Using a slotted spoon, transfer the meat into the well and top with the tfaia. Strain the cooking liquid from the meat and serve it separately as a sauce.

salads and vegetable side dishes

country salad with bell peppers and chiles

Fresh country salads vary according to the season but generally they are crunchy and tangy, and often packed with fresh herbs to cleanse the palate. A salad may be offered at the start of the meal to whet the appetite, or as an accompaniment to the heavier, syrupy tagines to cut the sweetness.

2 red onions, finely chopped

1 red bell pepper, seeded and chopped

1 green bell pepper, seeded and chopped

2 green chiles, seeded and chopped

2 celery ribs, chopped

2 garlic cloves, chopped

leaves from a large bunch each of fresh mint and flat-leaf parsley, chopped

2 tablespoons olive oil

freshly squeezed juice of ½ a lemon

sea salt and freshly ground black pepper

Serves 4

In a bowl, mix together the chopped onions, bell peppers, chiles, celery, garlic, mint, and parsley. Add the olive oil and lemon juice and season to taste with salt and pepper. Toss the salad throughly and serve immediately.

preserved lemon and tomato salad with capers

There are a variety of tomato-based salads that come under the banner *salade marocaine*, especially in the tourist areas. This particular recipe is a great favorite. Tart, fruity, crunchy, and refreshing, it appears in various versions throughout Morocco.

5–6 large tomatoes, skinned, seeded, and cut into thick strips

1 red onion, cut in half lengthwise, then in half crosswise, and sliced with the grain

rind of 1 preserved lemon, cut into thin strips (see page 11)

2–3 tablespoons olive oil

freshly squeezed juice of ½ lemon

1–2 tablespoons capers, rinsed and drained

leaves from a small bunch each of fresh flat-leaf parsley, cilantro, and mint, finely chopped

1 teaspoon paprika

sea salt and freshly ground black pepper

Serves 4-6

Put the tomatoes, onions, and preserved lemon in a bowl. Add the olive oil and lemon juice and toss well. Season to taste with salt and pepper and set aside until ready to serve.

Just before serving, toss in the capers and herbs and scatter the paprika over the top.

See photograph on page 123.

spicy eggplant and tomato salad

This classic spicy eggplant and tomato salad, which can be written as *zahlouk* or *zaalouk*, is delicious served on its own with chunks of bread, or as part of a spread. It can be made with olive oil or argan oil, which is pressed from the nut inside the fruit of the argan tree indigenous to the Souss region of Morocco.

* *

2 large eggplants

4 large tomatoes

½ scant cup olive or argan oil

2–3 garlic cloves, crushed

1 teaspoon harissa paste (see page 12)

leaves from a small bunch each of fresh flat-leaf parsley and cilantro, finely chopped

freshly squeezed juice of 1 lemon

sea salt and freshly ground black pepper

1 teaspoon cumin seeds, roasted and ground

crusty bread, to serve

Serves 4

Preheat the oven to 400°F.

Put the eggplants on a baking sheet and bake them in the preheated oven for about 30 minutes, until soft when you press them with a finger. Put the tomatoes in an ovenproof dish, pour over half the olive oil, and pop them in the oven to cook with the eggplants.

Remove the eggplants and tomatoes from the oven and leave until cool enough to handle. Using a sharp knife, cut the eggplants in half, scoop out the warm flesh, and chop it to a pulp. Skin the tomatoes, cut them in half, scoop out the seeds and chop the flesh to a pulp.

Heat the rest of the oil in a heavy-based pan, add the garlic and sauté until it begins to color, stirring constantly. Add the tomatoes and harissa and cook over a medium heat for 5–8 minutes, until thick and pulpy. Add the eggplants, parsley, and cilantro. Stir in the lemon juice and season to taste with salt and pepper. Tip into a serving bowl and serve warm or at room temperature with a dusting of roasted cumin and chunks of crusty bread.

roasted zucchini and apple salad with oranges

Zucchini is a popular summer vegetable in Morocco and, as it marries well with fresh herbs and garlic, it appears frequently in salads and dips as well as in vegetable and meat tagines. Served as an appetizer or as an accompaniment to a meat and poultry entrée, this salad is delightfully refreshing.

* *

2 medium zucchini, trimmed, cut in half crosswise and sliced lengthwise

1 green apple, cored, cut in half lengthwise and sliced crosswise

3 tablespoons olive oil

freshly squeezed juice of 1 lemon

1 tablespoon runny honey

2 sweet oranges, peeled with pith removed

rind of ½ preserved lemon, finely shredded (see page 11)

leaves from a small bunch of fresh mint, shredded

sea salt

Serves 4–6

Preheat the oven to 400°F.

Put the sliced zucchini and apple in an ovenproof dish and spoon over the oil. Cook in the preheated oven for about 20 minutes. Remove from the oven and pour over the lemon juice and honey. Return them to the oven for a further 10 minutes, until they have softened and are slightly golden in color. Leave them to cool in the dish.

Prepare the oranges on a plate to catch the juice. Slice them thinly into neat circles, remove any pips and arrange them on a serving dish. Spoon the roasted zucchini and apple on top of the oranges. Stir the orange juice that you have caught on the plate into the roasting juices in the baking dish and season with a little salt. Drizzle the juice over the salad and scatter the preserved lemon and mint over the top. Serve chilled or at room temperature.

chickpea salad with onions and paprika

Chickpeas, beans, and lentils are consumed daily in rural Morocco, particularly in areas where meat is scarce or expensive. They are cooked in stews, added to couscous, and find their way into salads. This dish is particularly good served warm and is often topped with crumbled goat cheese from the village.

* *

1½ cups dried chickpeas, soaked in plenty of cold water overnight

1 red onion, cut in half lengthwise, then in half crosswise, and sliced with the grain

4 garlic cloves, finely chopped

1 teaspoon ground cumin

1–2 teaspoons paprika

3 tablespoons olive oil

freshly squeezed juice of 1 lemon

leaves from a small bunch each of fresh flat-leaf parsley and cilantro, coarsely chopped

4 oz. firm goat cheese or feta, crumbled (optional)

sea salt and freshly ground black pepper

crusty bread, to serve

Serves 4

Drain the chickpeas and put them in a deep saucepan. Cover with water and bring to a boil. Reduce the heat and simmer for about 45 minutes, until the chickpeas are tender but not mushy. Drain the chickpeas and remove any loose skins—you can rub them in a clean kitchen towel, or between your fingers, to remove them.

Tip the warm chickpeas into a bowl. Add the onion, garlic, cumin, and paprika and toss in the olive oil and lemon juice while the chickpeas are still warm, making sure they are all well coated. Season with salt and pepper to taste and toss in most of the parsley and cilantro. Crumble over the goat cheese, if using, and sprinkle with the rest of the herbs. Serve while still warm with chunks of crusty bread.

sautéed spinach with orange and almonds

This dish is generally made with spinach or mallow, which grows wild in the countryside and is picked for vegetable dishes and soup. Quite often you will come across makeshift stalls selling bunches of mallow by the dusty roadside.

1 lb. fresh spinach leaves, thoroughly rinsed and drained

2–3 tablespoons olive oil plus a pat of butter

1 onion, roughly chopped

2 garlic cloves, finely chopped

freshly squeezed juice and peel of 1 orange

2 tablespoons slivered almonds, toasted

sea salt and freshly ground black pepper

Serves 2–4

Put the spinach in a steamer and cook for 8–10 minutes, until soft. Tip the cooked spinach onto a wooden board and chop to a pulp. Set aside.

Heat the oil and butter in a heavy-based saucepan. Stir in the onion and garlic and cook until they begin to color. Add the spinach and mix until thoroughly combined. Add the orange juice and peel and season to taste with salt and pepper. Tip the spinach into a serving dish and garnish with the toasted almonds.

braised fennel and zucchini with aniseed

Braised vegetables, such as zucchini and artichokes, are often combined with fruit or spices and served as an accompaniment to tagines or roasted meats. This recipe from Casablanca is aromatic rather than spicy and complements the fish tagines in this book.

3–4 tablespoons olive oil

2 fennel bulbs, trimmed and chopped

2 zucchini, trimmed and cut into cubes

1 tablespoon butter

2 teaspoons aniseeds

½ preserved lemon, very thinly sliced (see page 11)

sea salt and freshly ground black pepper

Serves 4

Heat the oil in a heavy-based saucepan and stir in the fennel. Cover with a lid and cook gently for 10–15 minutes. Stir in the zucchini and cook for a further 5 minutes, until they begin to soften.

Add the butter and the aniseeds and toss thoroughly. Season to taste with salt and pepper, sprinkle with the preserved lemon and serve immediately.

honey-glazed pumpkin with spices

Root vegetables and members of the squash family, such as sweet potatoes, turnips, butternut, and pumpkins, are often cooked with honey and spices as their sweet flesh remains succulent and marries well with these flavors. Generally, these sides are served with grilled or roasted meats.

* *

1¾ lbs. pumpkin flesh, with skin and seeds removed

3 tablespoons butter

2–3 tablespoons runny honey

2 cinnamon sticks

3–4 cloves

1 teaspoon ground ginger

½ teaspoon cayenne pepper

a small bunch of cilantro, finely chopped

sea salt and freshly ground black pepper

Serves 4

Preheat the oven to 350°F.

Put the pumpkin in a steamer and cook for about 10 minutes, until the flesh is tender but still firm. Tip the steamed flesh into an ovenproof dish.

Melt the butter in a saucepan and stir in the honey. Add the cinnamon sticks, cloves, ground ginger, and cayenne and season to taste with salt and pepper. Pour the mixture over the pumpkin then bake in the preheated oven for 15–20 minutes.

Tip the glazed pumpkin onto a serving plate, remove the cinnamon and cloves, then sprinkle with the cilantro. Serve warm as a side dish with roasted or grilled chicken or meat.

Moroccan ratatouille with dates

Similar to a French ratatouille, this delicious dish is spiked with a touch of *ras-el-hanout* and sweetened with succulent dates. Serve it with bread or Plain, Buttery Couscous or as an accompaniment to a tagine, grilled meats, or fish.

• •

4–5 tablespoons olive oil

1 onion, halved lengthwise and sliced crosswise

2 garlic cloves, chopped

1 red bell pepper, seeded and halved lengthwise and sliced crosswise

1 eggplant, halved lengthwise and sliced crosswise

2 zucchini, sliced

8 oz. ready-to-eat pitted dates, halved lengthwise

2 x 14-oz cans chopped tomatoes

1–2 teaspoons sugar

2 teaspoons ras-el-hanout (see page 15)

leaves from a small bunch of fresh flat-leaf parsley, coarsely chopped

sea salt and freshly ground black pepper

Plain, Buttery Couscous (see page 108), to serve (optional)

Serves 4–6

Heat the oil in a tagine or a heavy-based casserole dish. Add the onion and garlic and cook for 2–3 minutes until they begin to soften.

Add the bell pepper, eggplant, and zucchini and cook for a further 3–4 minutes. Add the dates, tomatoes, sugar, and ras-el-hanout and mix thoroughly. Cover and cook for about 40 minutes, until the vegetables are tender but not too soft.

Season to taste with salt and pepper and sprinkle the chopped parsley over the top. Serve hot with Plain, Buttery Couscous or as a vegetable accompaniment to a tagine, grilled meats, or fish.

melon and mint salad with orange flower water

This refreshing salad is an ideal accompaniment to spicy tagines. It is also served as a palate cleanser between the richly flavored tagine and the ensuing course of a plain or lightly flavored couscous.

1 ripe honeydew or galia melon, seeded and cut into bite-size chunks

leaves from a bunch of fresh mint, finely shredded (reserve a few whole leaves to garnish)

2 tablespoons orange flower water

1 tablespoon sugar or clear honey (optional)

Serves 4

In a bowl, toss the melon chunks with the mint and orange flower water, and sugar or honey, if using. Cover and chill in the refrigerator for 1–2 hours. Sprinkle with a few mint leaves and serve.

See photograph on page 139.

orange salad with red onion and black olives

Juicy salads made with citrus fruits, such as oranges and grapefruits, are very popular accompaniments to the spicier, and sometimes fiery hot, tagines. Colorful and refreshing, this salad is also delicious served with grilled and roasted meats.

3 fresh oranges, peeled with a knife to remove the pith, and thinly sliced

1 red onion, thinly sliced into rings

12 black olives, pitted

2–3 tablespoons olive oil

freshly squeezed juice of 1 lime

sea salt

1 teaspoon cumin seeds, roasted

½ teaspoon smoked paprika

leaves from a small bunch of cilantro, coarsely chopped

Serves 4

Arrange the orange slices on a serving dish or in a shallow bowl and place the onion slices and olives on top.

In a small bowl, whisk together the olive oil and lime juice and add salt to taste. Pour the dressing over the oranges. Sprinkle the cumin seeds, paprika, and cilantro leaves over the top and serve.

index

conversion chart

Volume equivalents:

American	Metric	Imperial
6 tbsp butter	85 g	3 oz.
7 tbsp butter	100 g	3½ oz.
1 stick butter	115 g	4 oz.
1 teaspoon	5 ml	
1 tablespoon	15 ml	
¼ cup	60 ml	2 fl.oz.
⅓ cup	75 ml	2½ fl.oz.
½ cup	125 ml	4 fl.oz.
⅔ cup	150 ml	5 fl.oz. (¼ pint)
¾ cup	175 ml	6 fl.oz.
1 cup	250 ml	8 fl.oz.

Oven temperatures:

120°C/130°C	(250°F)	Gas ½
140°C	(275°F)	Gas 1
150°C	(300°F)	Gas 2
160°C/170°C	(325°F)	Gas 3
180°C	(350°F)	Gas 4
190°C	(375°F)	Gas 5
200°C	(400°F)	Gas 6
220°C	(425°F)	Gas 7

Weight equivalents:

Imperial	Metric
1 oz.	30 g
2 oz.	55 g
3 oz.	85 g
3½ oz.	100 g
4 oz.	115 g
5 oz.	140 g
6 oz.	175 g
8 oz. (½ lb.)	225 g
9 oz.	250 g
10 oz.	280 g
11½ oz.	325 g
12 oz.	350 g
13 oz.	375 g
14 oz.	400 g
15 oz.	425 g
16 oz. (1 lb.)	450 g

Measurements:

Inches	Cm
¼ inch	0.5 cm
½ inch	1 cm
¾ inch	1.5 cm
1 inch	2.5 cm
2 inches	5 cm
3 inches	7 cm
4 inches	10 cm
5 inches	12 cm
6 inches	15 cm
7 inches	18 cm
8 inches	20 cm
9 inches	23 cm
10 inches	25 cm
11 inches	28 cm
12 inches	30 cm